THE UNFOLDING OF ARTISTIC ACTIVITY

NEGRO BOY SITTING IN MORNINGSIDE PARK
Done by a thirty-seven-year-old social worker

THE UNFOLDING OF ARTISTIC ACTIVITY

Its Basis, Processes, and Implications

BY HENRY SCHAEFER-SIMMERN

WITH A FOREWORD BY JOHN DEWEY

UNIVERSITY OF CALIFORNIA PRESS

BERKELEY AND LOS ANGELES ، 1970

UNIVERSITY OF CALIFORNIA PRESS
BERKELEY AND LOS ANGELES
CALIFORNIA

❖

UNIVERSITY OF CALIFORNIA PRESS, LTD.
LONDON, ENGLAND

SBN: 520-01141-4

Fourth printing, 1970

PRINTED IN THE UNITED STATES OF AMERICA

TO THE MEMORY OF

GUSTAF BRITSCH

1879-1923

FOREWORD

THE CONTRIBUTION *made in this volume to the philosophies of art and of education is notable from the standpoint of theory. At the same time, I believe that, important as is the contribution to both of these subjects, there is another one that is its most distinguished trait. It is that upon which emphasis falls in these introductory remarks. The principles in question are taken out of and beyond the territory of theoretical philosophy into the field of demonstrated fact. I shall, of course, have to confine what I say to the principles. But I should not be faithful to the book itself if I did not give first and foremost place to their testing and confirmation in work carried on over many years and with a variety of groups. This demonstration, reported in words and in pictorial evidence, gives substance and form to the principles that are set forth.*

The first of the principles to which I would call attention is the emphasis upon individuality as the creative factor in life's experiences. An immense amount has been said and written about the individual and about individuality. Too much of it, however, is vitiated by setting up what these words stand for as if it were something complete in itself in isolation. Here, it is seen and consistently treated as the life factor that varies from the previously given order, and that in varying transforms in some measure that from which it departs, even in the very act of receiving and using it. This creativity is the meaning of artistic activity—which is manifested not just in what are regarded as the fine arts, but in all forms of life that are not tied down to what is established by custom and convention. In re-creating them in its own way it brings refreshment, growth, and satisfying joy to one who participates.

Accompanying this principle, or rather inseparable from it, is the evidence that artistic activity is an undivided union of factors which, when separated, are called physical, emotional, intellectual, and practical—these last in the sense of doing and making. These last, however, are no more routine and dull than the emotional stir is raw excitation. Intelligence is the informing and formative factor throughout. It is manifested in that keen and lively participation of the sense organs in which they are truly organs of constructive imagination. Intelligence is also manifested in the organizing activity of which aesthetic form is the result. But nothing could be further away from that conformity to fixed rules, disguised as principles and standards, which is too often taken to be the function of "rationality." Escape from the one-sidedness which attends many philosophies of sense, of reason, of bodily or physical action, of emotion, and of doing and making, distinguishes the work reported upon in the following pages. In their place there is constant observation of the wholeness of life and personality in which activity becomes artistic.

Because of this wholeness of artistic activity, because the entire personality comes into play, artistic activity which is art itself is not an indulgence but is refreshing and restorative, as is always the wholeness that is health. There is no inherent difference between fullness of activity and artistic activity; the latter is one with being fully alive. Hence, it is not something possessed by a few persons and setting them apart from the rest of mankind, but is the normal or natural human heritage. Its spontaneity is not a gush, but is the naturalness proper to all organized energies of the live creature. Persons differ greatly in their respective measures. But there is something the matter, something abnormal, when a human being is forbidden by external conditions from engaging in that fullness according to his own measure, and when he finds it diverted by these conditions into unhealthy physical excitement and appetitive indulgence.

Normally and naturally, artistic activity is the way in which one may "gain in the strength and stature, the belief in his own powers, and the self-respect, which make artistic activity constructive in the growth of personality." It is this fact that distinguishes the demonstrations conducted by Professor Schaefer-Simmern. They take place in a particular field of activity as every form of experimental demonstration must do. But through that field, as well as in it, there is convincing thoroughgoing demonstration that activity which is artistic extends beyond all subjects conventionally named "The Fine Arts." For it provides the pattern and model of the full and free growth of personality and of full life activity, wherever it occurs, bringing refreshment and, when needed, restoration.

I am glad accordingly to close as I began—upon the note of effective demonstration of what is sound and alive in theoretical philosophies of art and of education.

JOHN DEWEY

PREFACE

IN THE *last quarter of the nineteenth century, the decline of artistic culture in central Europe impelled a few valuable attempts at definition of the basic meaning of artistic activity and of its realization in works of art. Conrad Fiedler, one of the great patrons of the time, concluded that "artistic activity begins when man, driven by an inner necessity, grasps with the power of his mind the entangled multiplicity of appearances and develops it into configured visual existence." This is common knowledge to all genuine artists, from their daily experience; yet in official art education it has been almost unknown and very seldom applied. It is to the merit of the late Gustaf Britsch that he verified Fiedler's ideas scientifically in his Theorie der bildenden Kunst. He shows that artistic activity as a "general attribute of the human mind" reveals itself, to a modest degree, in children's untutored drawings as well as in beginning stages of art of all times. He demonstrates the existence of definite evolutionary stages by which artistic configuration develops gradually from simple to more complex relationships of form. Thus he indicates a way toward the foundation of an art education which will encourage the natural unfolding of artistic activity as an inherent quality of man.*

My work in art education has been decisively stimulated by Britsch's theory. For twenty years I have tested his principles in practice, with children and adults, persons of different nationalities and of different mental, educational, and economic backgrounds. I have extended his theory and added to his findings. Out of this experience a doctrine of art education has emerged which may serve as a stimulus for new educational procedures and may activate latent, hitherto unconsidered, potentialities in artistic as well as other fields of human functioning. Moreover, such broadening of the layman's capabilities has definite social and cultural implications.

It seemed a natural step in the promotion of these ideas that they should find their first decisive American support in an organization dedicated to the "improvement of social and living conditions," the Russell Sage Foundation in New York City. This book presents the results of an experiment undertaken and financed by the Foundation for the purpose of showing by actual case histories the development of the creative potentialities in men and women in business and the professions, and in institutionalized delinquents and mental defectives; that is, in persons not devoted to the arts.

In presenting the artistic developments of various participants I was faced with the task of expressing by conceptual, verbal terms what had been experienced visually, and of arranging successively and logically factors which in reality were simultaneous and interrelated. I may, therefore, sometimes speak a language unfamiliar to the artist, to whom the artistic process is a well-known fact; and to the layman I may even speak of a process unknown to him, and in a language to which he is not accustomed. But these departures seem unavoidable in written statements like the present one. Knowing a picture from verbal description and grasping the picture visually are two completely different experiences. I should like to caution the reader against the rejection of unfamiliar concepts which stand for unfamiliar ideas. The important thing is to understand the processes for which the unfamiliar words are mere symbols.

I am greatly indebted to Dr. Allen Eaton, Director of the Department of Arts and Social Work of the Russell Sage Foundation. It was he who first saw the social implications of my work and prepared the way for introducing my experiment into the activities of the Foundation. He helped to organize the different projects, and throughout the four and a half years of my association with his department he was always generous with his advice. His constant belief in the ultimate value of what I was doing has contributed decisively to the final outcome. I also feel grateful to Dr. Shelby M. Harrison, General Director of the Russell Sage Foundation, whose approval made the experiment possible. I wish to thank Mr. Frederick R. Sacher, Superintendent of the New York City Reformatory in New Hampton, New York, and Mr. Ernest N. Roselle, Superintendent of the Southbury Training School in Southbury, Connecticut, for their permission to carry out this experiment in their institutions, and for their coöperation. I am grateful to Dr. Seymour Sarason, Chief Psychologist of the Southbury Training School and Assistant Professor of Psychology in Yale University, for his active participation and his report on his observations. To Dr. Rudolf Arnheim, of Sarah Lawrence College, I extend my sincere appreciation for suggestions that helped to clarify the psychological aspects of my work. I express my gratitude to Dr. Esther Lucile

Brown, Director of the Department of Studies on Professions of the Russell Sage Foundation, for helping to shape the manuscript. For invaluable advice and criticism I owe much to Dr. Martin Schütze, professor emeritus of the University of Chicago. To Professor John Dewey I can only very inadequately voice my thanks for the Foreword which he has so generously supplied. Finally, I wish to thank all my students, who created the material for this book.

H. S.-S.

University of California,
Berkeley, December, 1947.

ADDENDUM, 1961

NEARLY *thirteen years have passed since the first printing of this book. In the meantime, basic changes in the theory and practice of visual art that have been developing for several decades have become accepted contemporary trends. Some of the pictorial results are said to manifest "the free expression of the self," or the intuitive emergence of the artist's subconscious, or even to be visualizations of personal mystical revelations over which the artist has no control. Others do not pretend to be more than the display of emotional experiences. For the understanding and interpretation of any of these efforts, one can use only psychological and metaphysical approaches. Certain pictorial aspirations are affected by the new scientific discoveries and the corresponding new philosophical world-outlooks. To understand and interpret them, one must first of all grasp the scientific or philosophical suppositions which inspired them; but this means leaving the realm of visual perception, the true world of visual art, even if one intends later to return to it. Still other contemporary art trends seek status by the exaltation of one or another of the pictorial means pertaining to the artistic structure; they try for new discoveries in art by playful experi-mentalizing with line, mass, colors, planes; it is here that one finds "investi-gations into the spatial meaning of planes," and pictorial efforts that are said to exemplify "new theories of optics." And yet further, "there are twenty different systems or methods of abstract art"[1] alone. And "action painting" finds the significance of its works in the plastic realization of the artist's psycho-physical powers; his courage and his domination over his world are supposedly reflected in his forceful brushstrokes and large can-vases. Finally, there should be mentioned the attempts of modern art educa-tion to bring about the creation of something new by teaching ready-made, rationalized principles and rules of composition that lead to pictorial unifica-tions quite external to the "creator." To understand and to do justice to the*

---

[1] Michel Seuphor, *Dictionary of Abstract Painting* (New York: Tudor Publishing Co., 1957), p. 10.

meaning of such results, a knowledge of the underlying art-educational theory is required.

Obviously, a theory of art and art education which is concerned with the unfolding and development of an artistic language of form as an inherent mental attribute of every normal human being has nothing to offer to the interpretation of such pictorial results as have been mentioned above. The present-day trends rest upon ideologies, and stress approaches, with which the ideas set forth in this volume are substantially uncongenial. It is impossible to employ the ideas here presented if one is to give meaning to artistic phenomena so heterogeneous. And, vice versa, any attempt to approach the substance of this book from concepts of art and art education essentially alien to its intrinsic nature must inevitably misinterpret its meaning and importance. A distinct separation between the attitudes of today's art trends and the ideas presented here seems unavoidable if one is to assess either the one or the other at its proper value.

Those opponents of my ideas in art education who refuse to recognize them because they lack conformity with any contemporary theories of art should perhaps be reminded that I consider "education" still in its original meaning as "leading or drawing out" and not as "stuffing in." This educational attitude of mine—especially concerning art education—is substantiated by Gustaf Britsch's Theorie der bildenden Kunst, *which gives insights into the natural development of that mental faculty of man that enables him spontaneously to create interfunctional relationships of form in the realm of pure vision, independent of abstract rational thinking or of superimposed guidance. Only on this basis may the layman produce artistically in terms of his true nature. It would be difficult, if not impossible, to find in any of the theories underlying contemporary art trends the mental basis for such creativity.*

It should thus be clear that any attempt to "teach" the layman according to the rules of present-day art movements will be unsound artistically as well as educationally. In the course of my thirty-five years in the field of art education I have seen over and over again the disastrous effects of teaching-methods, aiming mainly at external production, which resort to current notions with which the student's own artistic conceptions are little or not at all congenial. In fact such influences are likely to bring forward individuals, split mentally and emotionally, whose inner lack of security is armored in the triple brass of an arrogance that for them is protective but to others is insufferable. Instead of being in full accord with their work, they are subjected to great nervous tensions. This, of course, stands in utter contrast to the purposes of the present volume. The mental, emotional, and physical synthesis of man, his healthy functional wholeness, is the final aim of my educational efforts. Only that kind of art activity which is intrinsically related to man's nature can serve that aim.

My work with lay students has frequently been criticized because it lacks a bent toward nonobjective art, which to my critics is "the only art that symbolizes the mind of contemporary man." It has been said in justification of the works of those artists who produce nonobjective art that the world, so far as they are concerned, is "irrevocably exhausted"; but it is not thus exhausted for the layman. Though his artistic vision is stimulated by the objects of the visible world, the beginnings of his artistic activity, regardless of how simple they may be, are not imitative, not merely expressive, but creative in the sense of producing spontaneously an interfunctional, self-sustained relationship of form. Similarly as in the artistic productions of primitive man, in genuine folk art, and in the unadulterated pictorial activity of children, "the essence of the world which he tries to appropriate mentally and to subjugate to himself consists in the visible and tangible Gestalt-formation of its objects."² To him, "art does not start from abstract thought in order to arrive at forms; rather it climbs from the formless to the formed, and in this process is found its entire mental meaning."³ There is no need of introducing to the layman another approach for his pictorial activity when already his innate, spontaneous approach can be basically creative.

I have repeatedly been accused of deliberately cultivating an artistic primitivism, and this in a highly sophisticated world that is everywhere dominated by scientific investigations. My critics seem to have forgotten that my entire art-educational program is built upon the idea of "the unfolding of artistic activity" and not upon the teaching of ready-made formulas for the fabrication of works of art. "Unfolding," however, can only start from a primary state of being from which a gradual development can take place

---

² Conrad Fiedler, *On Judging Works of Visual Art* (2d ed.; University of California Press, 1957), p. 43. Fiedler is here speaking of "the artist"; but what he has to say applies also to "the layman" in the sense proper to the present discussion.

³ *Ibid.*, p. 49.

in accordance with definite stages of growth. Primary, primitive, stages within artistic unfolding are therefore not only indispensable, but are the only guarantee of a normal, natural growth of that activity. The inborn creative potentialities of many persons are of course limited; these individuals may remain always in primary states of artistic awareness. There is nothing wrong with this. Their primary, primitive, artistic achievements are the natural outcome of their talents, and are humanly and artistically genuine. The artistic language of the people has always been a primary one in comparison with the artistic language of the masters; nevertheless, it has always been the backbone of the artistic culture of the people. The apparent structural similarity in the beginning of visual configurations in the artistic productions of laymen is due to an undifferentiated way of visually conceiving relationships of form. With more differentiation of these relationships, more differentiated structures appear and more individual expression becomes possible. This phenomenon can be plainly seen in the development of art in all epochs as well as in primitive and folk art.

In some references to my work as presented in this book it has been stated that I am fostering "visual memory" in order to make possible the attainment of visual configuration. This is a basic misinterpretation of my ideas. The cause of the misleading statement lies in practices common to present-day art education, practices that derive from the illusion that interfunctional relationships of form—visual configuration—can be attained by urging the student to "reproduce the visually present subject," and that "ultimately he becomes creatively productive only when he is able to call forth, from memory, a visual 'configuration' to serve his expressive purposes." Nowhere in this volume has such a practice ever been mentioned. It is the misinterpretation that needs a thorough clarification.*

Visual memory tries to remember (indeed, to "re-member") the external shapes of objects in a piecemeal way. Asking how this or that part of the object may look, how it may be connected with other parts, how large or small, thick or thin it may be, in what proportions it stands to its surroundings, calls for the help of rational calculation, and not for visual conceiving. In so doing it puts parts of objects together without any interfunctional relationship of the shapes to each other. The outcome is a "re-membering," a putting together of disjunct members, isolated details; parts

---

[4] Frederick M. Logan, *Growth of Art in American Schools* (New York: Harper & Brothers, 1955), p. 257.

can be changed without affecting the whole. Such weak structures, arranged willfully in order to re-collect various members of objects, can never lead to the establishment of visual configurations. The drawing of a tree here illustrated in picture A is an example of an image resulting from visual memory. Just the opposite is shown in picture B;[5] the whole structure of this drawing

A   B

of a tree reveals a definite visual order in the relationship of all parts to each other. First, the whole tree and all its details are set off from the empty white background, and thus the drawing attains a unified flatness all over. Further, the main shape, consisting of tree trunk and large and smaller branches, discloses a visual pattern built upon a relationship of definite slanting angles that determine also the relationship of leaves to twigs; and thus one direction of lines leads into the direction of lines adjoining, so that the eye of the observer is guided to grasp the total image. If a change is undertaken in any part, either in the relationship of the figure to its empty background or in the definite relationship of the directions of the slanting lines, the whole drawing loses the particular quality of its configuration.

By now it should be clear that such a self-sustained unity of form-relation-

[5] It should be noted that this example represents only one particular stage of visual configuration corresponding to an early stage of artistic development.

ships can never be the result of visual memory. Rather, one is compelled to recognize that specific power in the mind of man by virtue of which he is able to create such a configuration of form—the artistic form—which in turn leads to the artistic interpretation. The spontaneous creation of the artistic form, its unfolding and development as an intrinsic attribute of every normal human being, is the very substance of this volume.

I should like to express my gratitude to Dr. Rudolf Arnheim of Sarah Lawrence College, who is also Professor of Psychology at the New School for Social Research, and to Dr. Seymour Sarason, Professor of Psychology at Yale University, both of whom have generously referred to the importance of my work in their own publications. To all art educators who have used this book as an inspiration for their endeavors—making this third printing necessary—I humbly voice my thankfulness.

H. S.-S.

Berkeley, California,
March, 1961.

CONTENTS

Introductory Remarks and Statement of Theory

Chapter One

THE NEED FOR CREATIVE EXPERIENCE

MANY PHASES of human activity, in modern civilization, are mechanized and specialized. The "machine age" has increased the comforts of daily living, but the nonmechanical needs of man's nature have been less and less met. As industrial production has been speeded up, more free time has become available, and many persons have used it in pursuance of their valuable interests; but thousands of others have been thrown into idleness.

Now, increased mechanization, specialization, and leisure have a decisive influence upon the destiny of our future civilization. Modern industry, having decreased the need for trained craftsmanship, has reduced many working processes to the level of routine manipulation. In natural ways of working, man acts as a psychophysical whole, his intellectual, emotional, and physical forces operating in a coördinated fashion. In mechanical manipulation, hands, feet, and eyes work relatively isolated from the core of man's interest, and the performance, therefore, is not related to his essential nature. Constant compulsory isolation of functions must inevitably endanger the individual's equilibrium.

Acquisition and accumulation, both material and intellectual, have become predominant measures of value. Lack of material success stamps the individual as inadequate. Values have become more external, and even in intellectual fields mere accumulation of knowledge has been overemphasized. In present-day education, intellectual materialism is stressed. As a consequence, man is only partly educated and only partly a functioning entity. Because the harmonious development of his sensuous, emotional, intellectual, and physical powers is neglected, his creative capacities cannot unfold.

This is one of the reasons why only a small minority of the population is able to use its increased leisure time for constructive purposes, while the majority dissipates it in idleness. However, in periods of need man calls forth latent powers to maintain his balance. The increased interest in sports at the end of the nineteenth century exemplified a determination to counteract exploitation by the machine. But never before did the problem of free time become so serious as in the years of unemployment, the late 'twenties and early 'thirties. Never did the need of defending human worth seem so imperative as in those days of indignity and degradation.

It is significant that the most thoroughly industrialized country, the one with the most progressive mechanized system, undertook the greatest effort to conserve human integrity. The establishment of the Works Progress Administration was a decisive step in this direction. It is no coincidence that the W. P. A. Art Project ranks among the highest means utilized for maintaining and strengthening man's creative consciousness. Never before has any nation shown such foresight in recognizing artistic activity as an instrument for the restoration of human dignity. Thousands of day and night classes, in which different techniques and the uses of different media were taught, were opened to persons of all ages. The Federal Government also encouraged and made possible the continuation of the artist's own work. In the larger cities, organized art associations, museums, settlement houses, and the Young Men's and Young Women's Christian Associations, further fostered artistic interest.

Many other organizations have acknowledged the importance of art expression for their members as a necessary balance against the routine of daily occupations. For example, the International Ladies' Garment Workers' Union conducts art classes twice a week. There are businessmen's art clubs in almost a dozen American cities. In the midst of the economic depression a New York Physicians' Art Club was established, and five years later it had almost a hundred active members. An American Physicians' Art Club has been founded, with headquarters in San Francisco.

Art as an element in rural homemaking has been fostered by the Extension Service of the United States Department of Agriculture. As many as two thousand home demonstration agents were, at one time, employed to stimulate interest in design and color in clothing, house furnishing, home arts and crafts, and the appreciation of good music and pictures. Hundreds of other organizations and clubs, large and small, have made noteworthy efforts to awaken creative potentialities. Although the W. P. A. Art Project was dissolved, many of the other enterprises still exist.

Now, having in mind the importance of awakening man's artistic abilities as a weapon against the danger of the mechanization and disintegration of his life, it seems essential to throw some light upon the methods hitherto used for this purpose.

A study of the teaching methods put into practice in classes for children and adolescents shows a wide preference for the doctrine of self-expression. In contrast to older principles, such as copying, or following imposed techniques, this pedagogical attitude has definite values. It accepts the child as a personality with "inherent abilities to see, to feel, and to express life." Leaving him free in his pictorial efforts is the basic educational principle. The child usually enjoys it. Energies are released which give him the feeling of creating something. To the psychologist and psychiatrist this kind of self-expression offers insight into various important psychological processes—a fact which explains why such investigators are less interested in the artistic quality of the child's work than in drawing and painting as a "projective technique." Nevertheless, this "laissez-faire" procedure has many disadvantages. Finger paintings and watercolors painted with big brushes in a fraction of an hour may exhibit many facets of the child's personality, but "what is sometimes called an art of self-expression might better be termed one of self-exposure, it discloses character—or lack of character—to others. In itself it is only a spewing forth."[1] At adolescence, critical judgment has usually so far progressed that the young student refuses to recognize his pictorial achievements of self-expression as conforming with his stage of mental development. He loses interest, and thus his pictorial powers diminish. Hence, the educational method which aims at self-expression, though it may have psychological values, does not forward the growth of the child's artistic abilities.

In order to overcome the deficiencies of merely "self-expressive" spontaneous activity in the visual arts, the customary pedagogical practice is to attempt to mold the abilities of the adolescent toward the attainments of the "Masters." In effect, this aim is to induce him to produce pictorially on a level that may be beyond his comprehension and that has no relationship to his personality. A seeming likeness between his work and that of an adult artist guarantees neither artistic quality nor personal satisfaction. It is beyond the reach of the less gifted and gives a feeling of false superiority to the talented.

Most adults are unaware of their creative potentialities. If they have done

---

[1] John Dewey, *Art as Experience* (New York: Minton, Balch, 1934), p. 62.

something in the visual arts, their work has consisted mainly in imitation of nature. Usually they are taught to follow the "style" of their instructors. Here are to be found many of the well-known procedures which characterize present-day art teaching. Some types of instruction sail openly under old academic banners, some are camouflaged by modernistic slogans; either way, external achievement is primarily taken into account, while the student's personal conception is often neglected. All the various art trends, as for instance the academic, impressionistic, expressionistic, abstract, and lately the surrealistic, are reflected in corresponding principles of art education. These principles determine the methods of teaching in special as well as in general schools. They even penetrate into leisure-time art instruction. They set the measures of value by which the works of the rising generation are "judged and altered." Unfortunately, they imply that artistic activity is not a natural attribute of human nature; rather, that it must be acquired by industrious efforts at adapting the preconceived ideas of others. But genuine artistic abilities cannot thus develop; instead, man's inborn creative potentialities are strangled within him.

Since external accomplishments are stressed, the further course of such teaching often reduces the artistic process to mere surface decoration; there is no organic unfolding of the student's own artistic ability; he becomes, in any field of pictorial production, a victim of unrelated specialization. Usually, the formal structures of his drawings have no connection with those of his paintings, and they in turn are alien to his designs. He does not experience the inner relationship of the so-called fine and applied arts, of crafts and industrial arts. Since they do not emerge out of his own creative being, they do not have personal meaning to him. His participation in imitative art classes may be "fun," and he may take pleasure in acquiring facility in the various modes of expression, but he does not gain in the strength and stature, the belief in his own powers, and the self-respect which would make artistic activity constructive in the growth of his personality. On the contrary, specialization within the pictorial processes forces him into further complication. He becomes divided within himself.

This brief survey of the principles of art education now generally practiced may point to their ineffectiveness in cultivating constructive human forces to counteract the influences of an overmechanized and materialistic life. How can the methods most commonly used bring about the desired results if they do not establish a natural, inner relationship between man and his work, and if, furthermore, they contain in themselves the same characteristic as the evils of social disintegration which they ought to remedy? These doctrines of art teaching emphasize the same detailed systematization and specialization that are found in the daily work of those who are seeking their human value through the awakening of their creative potentialities.

This type of teaching, whether it aims at old or supermodern accomplishments, is based upon a traditional psychology of perception which considers an outwardly arranged composition derived from various separated external stimuli and sensations as the essential factor in the construction of works of visual art. Thus, it overlooks the assumption of inherent powers of artistic configuration as an attribute of human nature. It grows out of the so-called "atomistic" method, which has its origin in the culture and economic structure of the nineteenth century. "Atomism" tried to reach an understanding of processes and events by overevaluating and isolating details. It succeeded in achieving enormous specialized knowledge in various fields, but simultaneously it tended to lose comprehension of total relationships; hence it led to further dissolution and contributed to separating man more and more from a natural way of life.

Only by trying to grasp processes in their totality, in which single phenomena are indivisibly related to the meaning of the whole, may one reach a better understanding of life. The unfolding of artistic activity cannot be separated from the nature of man; it must grow out of him as a unified process. The essence of his being should determine its course. Only then will it become a force in the upbuilding of a world that is adequate to his nature.

Chapter Two

NEW DIRECTIONS

THE PRECEDING chapter indicated that new directions in art education are essential to meet the need for creative experience and that they must be based upon the natural unfolding and development of artistic abilities. Art education which seeks this goal should find a new orientation and determine the conditions under which it can fulfill its task.

A work of art manifests various aspects of human nature and therefore can be approached from various viewpoints: the philosophical, the religious, the psychological, the social, the technical, among others. Each of these may entitle the observer to define his own concept of any work of art. It is on the basis of *pictorial data only,* however, that the present writer would define those characteristics which may be used to distinguish a work of art from any other pictorial production. The substance of this study, he hopes, will demonstrate that an attempt thus governed, which is independent of subjective opinions, of "likes and dislikes," will best suffice to reveal the nature of a work of art.

A work of visual art, then, which includes the general human aspects referred to above can be distinguished from any other pictorial production by a functional interrelationship of all its parts. This visual configuration may be considered the result of an autonomous mental activity, a mental digestion and transformation of sensory experience into a newly created visual entity. It should be emphasized—and it will later be demonstrated—that this activity is independent of conceptual intellectual calculation and that it takes place solely within the realm of visual experience. Its result may be defined as a sensory creation. This visual configuration, which may be termed the *artistic form,* is the artist's language by which he expresses his ideas visually and artistically. It is the artistic form that realizes a specific experience as an artistic experience and that symbolizes its creator's artistic consciousness. It is the artistic form by which any content of representation becomes an artistic content. Thus, form and content cannot be separated from each other; they are an indivisible unity.

Artistic form is usually recognized only where it appears in highly evolved works of art. However, it can also be found in simple beginnings, such as the pictorial achievements of prehistoric man and of primitive tribes, in folk art, and in the spontaneous drawings and sculptures made by children. Recent studies—starting with those of the late Gustaf Britsch and continued by his followers, including the author—have revealed that children's drawings not yet distorted by external methods of teaching or by imitation of nature possess a definite structural order which in essence is similar to that of more developed works of art. This configuration not only expresses general human attributes, but also embodies them in an indissoluble relationship of form, a "constancy of form." This unified structure, simple though it is, may be recognized as the "seed" of the artistic form.

Experiments have shown that, keeping pace with the developing mind of the normal individual, there develops also an organic growth of visual artistic configurations. Simple structures of form have been found to precede more complicated ones, thus indicating the natural way in which artistic abilities unfold and develop. One should not expect most children or adults to reach the most highly organized levels of artistic achievement, any more than one expects that the ordinary student of science in school will become a great scientist. It must be emphasized, however, that all normal human beings, and subnormal, too, possess in some degree the ability to produce genuinely artistic works. And just as conceptual thinking can minister to the integration of personality, so inherent artistic abilities can and should be utilized.

At this point, a brief presentation of the underlying theory is required. The theory attempts to reveal the nature of artistic activity, its organic development and growth, and further, to establish the fact that artistic activity is a function of general human activity, and to indicate its relation to ordinary experience. It must be noted that this theory does not start from any ready-made conception of art. It is based upon scientific examinations of works of art of all different epochs and races.

One of the most primitive stages of man's pictorial production, illustrated by children's drawings, is represented by simple outlined figures that have

---

[1] Kurt Koffka, *The Growth of the Mind* (New York: Harcourt, Brace, 1925), p. 295. Koffka was one of the first to discover such configurations in the early beginnings of a child's pictorial activity. He pointed to the fact that this activity should be attributed to definite laws of perception.

the approximate shape of circles (picture 1). Because of the child's inability to control his motor behavior, his drawings have irregular outlines, but they tend to be more or less round. Whereas his earliest scribbles are mere traces of motor activity, the circles are the result of a visual activity directed toward the production of a definite form. They may therefore be called "intentional

Courtesy of the Harriet Johnson Nursery School, New York City

1. Drawing by a three-year-old child.

figures." There is already a definite relationship between each intentional "figure" and its surroundings or "ground."[2] Figure cannot exist without ground. This indissoluble union marks the most primitive beginning of artistic configuration—of artistic form. To verify the fundamental importance of the figure-ground relationship one need only call to mind that figure and ground can also be distinguished in other modes of experience: in speaking, thinking, feeling. "A word, for instance, is understandable only within a definite context, within a definite sentence, within a certain cultural sphere. Habitually we ignore the background and pay attention only to the figure.

---

[2] These terms have been introduced in the psychology of perception by Edgar Rubin, in *Visuell Wahrgenommene Figuren* (Copenhagen, 1931).

From the standpoint of systematic observation and methodology this is false, for figure and ground are intimately interconnected. Neither can be properly evaluated without the other."[3]

The intentional figure which originally, as a circle, had no extension in any direction, next becomes extended either vertically or horizontally, or simul-

2. Schematic representation of children's drawings, showing the stage of visual conceiving in accordance with the greatest contrast of direction of lines.

taneously in both directions (picture 2). The simple line, the essential element of the intentional figure, may be amplified in the shape of an outlined, directed plane; in an outlined, directed plane connected with strokes; or in a combination of directed strokes. In this way the figure obtains an orderly structure based upon the greatest contrast of direction. All parts are related to one another by the horizontal-vertical order. Not one line can be changed without disturbing the structural organization of form. If a change is undertaken in one part, it demands also a change in the others in order to maintain the unity

[3] Kurt Goldstein, *Human Nature* (Harvard University Press, 1940), p. 13.

of form. Only in their relation to the whole do the parts obtain structural meaning. Furthermore, each single part is clearly discriminated from every other part. The relationship of the greatest contrast of direction of lines and the relationship of figure and ground constitute, together, an inseparable totality of form.

3. Schematic representation of children's drawings, showing the stage of visual conceiving in accordance with variability of direction of lines.

It is clear that drawings thus produced are not reproductions of particular aspects of the objects represented. Nor can they be considered as the pictorial realizations of abstract concepts or of reproductive memory. That a child knows a horse has four legs, or a human being two arms and two legs, by no means explains the definite configuration of form within the construction. That it does not explain it is demonstrated by the fact that children at this stage of development draw running animals by giving them additional legs. What the child depicts is something completely new. For the variety and multiplicity of shapes in nature he creates a definite organization of form by which he comprehends the world visually.⁴ His drawings, therefore, must be evaluated as independent visual entities. Their existence can be explained only

---

⁴ The term "create" is used in this book to designate the autonomous mental activity of transforming visual experience into artistic form.

as the result of a definite mental activity of conceiving relationships of form in the realm of pure vision—an activity that may be called "visual conceiving" and its pictorial realization, which is "visual conception." The term visual conception is used in a literal sense, to designate that which is conceived or

4. Drawing by a nine-year-old child.

begotten in the mind and which causes the birth of a visual configuration of form, that is, the *artistic form*. Mental activity that transforms the multiplicity of visual impressions into self-created visual unities leads to visual cognition.[5]

In the stage of visual conception that has just been described, objects are visually comprehended by means of the greatest contrast of direction of lines, combined with the previously demonstrated figure-ground relationship. In

---

[5] Visual cognition is the result of an immediate mental digestion of visual experience into a visual synthesis of form; it is not the result of an accumulation, registration, or reproduction of mere facts by means of conceptual activity.

the course of the development of visual conceiving, the direction of lines is changed; and this new variability of direction is again governed by a unity of direction in which all lines become members, and thus the whole figure attains a new structural organization of form. (Picture 3.) Now it becomes

5. Drawing by a thirteen-year-old child.

possible to distinguish between movements and stationary attitudes, a fact which proves that expression of movement is a result of a definite stage of visual conceiving; that is, it is a product of visual cognition.

The stage of variability of direction controlled by an organically developing principle of unity is a stage that becomes gradually more differentiated. Branches obtain smaller branches which are attached to one another by similar angles, limbs are divided and their parts are also related by similar angles (picture 4). Step by step, application of this principle to the whole figure expresses more and more vitality (picture 5). Again it must be noted that this vitality, inherent in a more complicated order of form, cannot be achieved by imitation of nature. It is the result of a gradual unfolding and development of man's inherent evolutionary processes of visual conceiving and cannot be separated from the artistic form. Vitality of expression, which

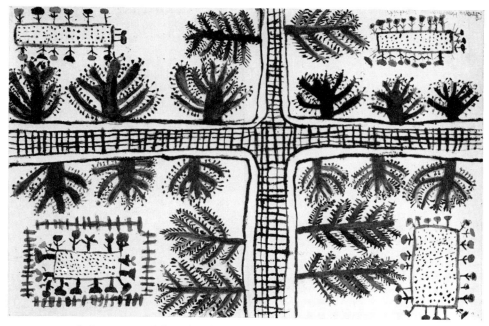

6. Crossing roads bordered by trees. Painted by a ten-year-old child.

has just been shown to be a relatively complicated configuration of form, illustrates conversely why works of art produced in the earlier stages of artistic activity, in which visual conception is still undifferentiated, are characterized by a certain apparent "stiffness and lifelessness."

Thus far, unity of direction has governed only the parts of a single figure and has not concerned a larger complex of figures. However, it is understandable that within a larger pictorial formation in which the primary figure-ground relationship still exists and in which the placing of figures is determined by other figures with which they belong, the previous relationship of forms, the horizontal-vertical, may still be employed (picture 6). The borders of the roads in our picture (which themselves are outlined figures)

7. Drawing water from a pond bordered by trees. Egyptian mural painting of about 1500 B.C.

represent the base lines toward which trees and flowers are vertically directed. This structural formation cannot be considered, therefore, as if trees and flowers were drawn upside down, but must be recognized as the pictorial realization of a particular stage of visual conception. The following examples from Egyptian, Persian, and American folk art (pictures 7, 8, and 9) verify the frequent occurrence of this artistic phenomenon in the art of times past.

After total coherence of direction in single figures has been fully grasped,

8. Persian-garden carpet of the seventeenth century.

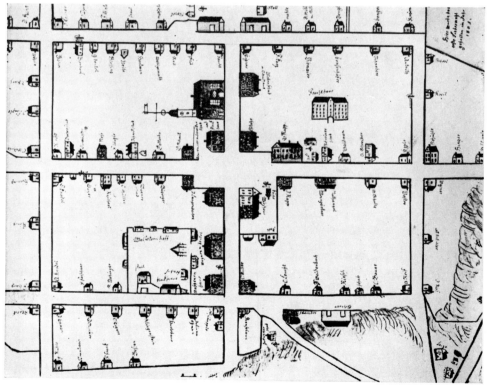

Courtesy of the American German Review, *October, 1941*

9. Map of Harmony, Pennsylvania, drawn by W. Weingartner, 1833.

the principle can be applied to any number of figures. All trees and flowers now "grow upward" in one direction from the earth (picture 10).

In the evolution of all mental activities, simple functions slowly blend into more complicated ones. Thus, early structural forms and later ones often appear side by side. This juxtaposition may occur within single figures, in which

10. Park pond surrounded by trees. A painting on red cardboard done coöperatively by two thirteen-year-old boys.

the stage of the greatest contrast of direction can be found together with the form of the succeeding stage of variability of direction. It appears frequently in pictures with many figures. One may therefore speak of transitional stages.

When a highly differentiated object increases the difficulty of the creation of visual configuration, the human mind often regresses to a less complicated stage of visual conceiving in order to attain visual comprehension. For instance, a picture of trees with many branches and leaves may still show the characteristic of the primary, outlined and directed, intentional figure; the picture is thus drawn in order to obtain a clear figure-ground relationship whereby, in turn, the parts can be grasped as a whole (picture 11). Regression to an earlier stage may occur at any artistic level. The configuration accomplished by regression has its origin in the drive for attainment of visual cognition.

In all early works of art in which the demonstrated stages are clearly apparent, figures are organized side by side and above and below one another

11. Drawing by an eleven-year-old child.

without interference. (See picture 10.) Even spatial depth is determined and defined by a structural organization in one plane. Figures are not arranged one "behind" another, because that kind of arrangement would distort the clear structural upbuilding of a figure and would affect the figure-ground relationship. Consequently, where spatial depth is meant, figures are organized "above" one another. Where a base line has been drawn as an indication of a level upon which figures are standing, a new base line above these figures is necessitated. A further sign of depth is demonstrated by a gradual diminution in the size of figures toward the upper part of the picture. (See picture 12.)

12. Landscape. Watercolor by a ten-year-old boy.

An even more advanced way of representing depth appears to be derived directly from the stage of variability of direction. In picture 13 (of a birdhouse in a tree) the front of the birdhouse is constructed by horizontal and vertical lines which have a relationship of direction to each other. The structure of the top and side of the birdhouse show an application of the principle of variability

13. Birdhouse in tree. Drawing by a twelve-year-old child.

of direction of lines: an angle similar to those which relate the branches of the tree to one another extends from the right vertical edge and likewise from the top horizontal edge of the front of the birdhouse. But whereas the branches show only a relationship of variability of direction of lines, the structure of the side and top of the birdhouse shows the variability of direction of lines governed by a relationship (parallelism) of direction of lines. The structure thus made demonstrates that slanted lines can be used not only to represent acute or obtuse angles within a plane, but also, in combination with rectangles, to give the impression of a new dimension of spatial depth.

So far, the term "stage" has been used to characterize the successive steps in the organic growth of man's visual conception as the mental foundation of artistic activity. It is now necessary to emphasize that no organic stages can be found in common reproduction or imitation. Spatial depth, for instance, can also be accomplished by nonartistic means—by mere application of fixed rules for perspective, or by superficial imitation; in other words, by conceptual calculation or reproductive memory. In such "artistic" exercises the essence of artistic activity, that is, the pictorial realization of visual conceiving,

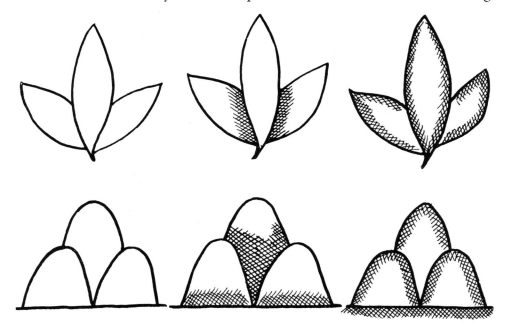

14. Schematic representation illustrating borderless transition from parts with figural meaning to parts with ground meaning, a stage in visual conceiving.

is not recognized. In the organic unfolding of artistic activity, a more highly developed degree of spatial depth can be achieved only by a more complicated stage of visual conceiving.

With the greater differentiation within single figures, as well as with the increase of the number of objects in a picture, figures tend to touch. Each original relationship of figure and ground is then affected, and a new figure-ground relationship between adjacent figures must be established. The following example may illustrate this problem.

In the stage of figure-ground relationship considered earlier, exemplified in picture 5, each outlined leaf is clearly bordered against its ground and carries figural meaning. In the upper left-hand figure of picture 14, only the center leaf is entirely outlined and possesses figural meaning. The other leaves have figural meaning only where they are outlined and bordered against the background of the paper. Where they are not outlined, they carry ground meaning for the center leaf. In sum, the areas of the outlined leaves to left and right of the center leaf contain both figural meaning and ground meaning. Their parts with figural meaning go over, borderless, into parts with ground meaning. The lower left-hand figure of the same illustration (picture 14), of two hills overlapping a third hill, presents the same problem and solution. The areas close to the outlines of the hills carry figural meaning, which in turn goes borderless over into areas that carry ground meaning for the adjacent parts. The base line upon which the hills rest is not a part of the hills, but represents the border of earth beneath and therefore has figural meaning. Through this new relationship of form, figures are clearly set behind or in front of one another. The parts with ground meaning bring out distinctly the neighboring parts with figural meaning. There is a new functional interrelationship through which they are joined inextricably together. It is this new stage of visual conceiving, the stage of the borderless transition from parts with figural meaning to parts with ground meaning, through which the phenomenon of overlapping gives way to a new idea of spatial depth.

For the purpose of stressing this new structural function of the borderless transition, either parts with figural meaning or those with ground meaning may be shaded, thereby making the borderless transition appear in a visually more comprehensible way. (See center and right-hand figures of picture 14.) A more distinct feeling of "in front" and "behind" is gained, whereby spatial depth attains stronger effect. In this stage, the phenomenon of shadow and light enters the artistic process. However, it must be noted that shadow and light can also be a result of imitation. Only when shadow and light obtain a functional value within a definite relationship of form do they belong to the realm of visual art. Furthermore, when the shaded parts of figure or ground are realized by color, the borderless transition requires a gradual nuance of color tones. Transition by means of color represents an important step in the acquisition of a new conception—the beginning of painting. As is well known, the unadulterated drawings of children, as well as entire sections of primitive and early art, such as Egyptian art, do not contain shadow and light, to say nothing of highlights. In them, the precondition for visual conception out of

15. (*Left*) Detail of a Chinese painting of the Sung period, 960–1270 A.D. The figural meaning of the outlined rocks goes gradually over into their shaded parts, which take on the pictorial function of ground meaning with respect to the neighboring rocks.

16. (*Below*) Detail of an Indian miniature painting of the seventeenth century. The structure of the rocks is again as in picture 15; but the outlines of the animals, as well as their limbs, have shaded figural meaning which goes gradually over into light ground meaning with respect to their adjacent parts.

17. Detail of a Flemish tapestry of about 1500 A.D. The shaded upper parts of hills go gradually over into light areas which assume the pictorial function of ground meaning with respect to the lower parts, and the figural meaning of the outlined leaves goes gradually over into their shaded parts which take on ground meaning with respect to the neighboring leaves.

Pictures 15–17 courtesy of the Metropolitan Museum of Art, New York City

which shadow and light can grow as a factor in artistic formation has not yet
been reached. It is again evident that the artistic phenomenon of shadow
and light is the result of a definite stage of visual conceiving, the stage of the
borderless transition from parts with figural meaning to parts with ground
meaning.

The attainment of this level reveals an appreciable maturity of artistic
ability. It is not usual before adolescence. The principle of form by which it
is characterized represents a most important enrichment of artistic expression.
Its remarkable creative possibilities are impressively illustrated in great periods
of art, such as early Chinese landscape painting, the art of the Middle Ages,
and Indian and Persian paintings of the sixteenth and seventeenth centuries.
(See pictures 15, 16, and 17.)

In the unfolding of inborn artistic abilities of most persons, it will be
almost impossible to reach the still more highly differentiated stages of artistic configuration. Hence it seems superfluous to attempt a discussion of
their structural function. In the history of art they are demonstrated by the
art of the High Renaissance and the Baroque, as well as by that of Impres-
sionism.

The role that color plays within the structural order of a work of art is also
conditioned by the stage of development of visual conceiving. Analogously
to the early stage of the greatest contrast of direction, pure colors stay also
in the greatest contrast to each other. Just as the visual conceiving of the
horizontal-vertical relationship progresses gradually to the more differentiated
one of variability of direction, visual conceiving of pure colors leads also to
more differentiated relationships of color nuances. Just as, in the stage of
variability of directions, the whole figure is controlled by a unity of direction
(see the upward-directed tree in picture 3), and just as this relationship is
transferred to a larger complex (see the unified upward direction of *all* the
trees in picture 10), so, in the field of color, harmony of color nuances is
achieved. Further, just as borderless transition from parts with figural meaning to parts with ground meaning creates a new unified organization of form,
so does the analogous transition in the realm of color create a new integration
in the color structure of a picture. The greatest advance in the use of a differentiated color scheme is exemplified in the artistic achievements of the great
Impressionists: light, air, and atmosphere entered the artistic process and
opened a completely new approach to visual cognition of the world.

The highly differentiated coloration found in the works of the great Impressionists tended to surpass the limits of visual perception. The taking over of the external technique of these masters by their many followers, and the rise of the imitative-realistic attitude, at the end of the nineteenth and the beginning of the twentieth century, led artistic activity into mere surface decoration. As a consequence, an inner need for regaining lost artistic values has emerged in recent decades and many works of modern art manifest real artistic qualities. A striking phenomenon in many of these works is their revelation of early stages of visual conceiving in their structural formation (in the works of Cézanne, Matisse, Derain, and Picasso, for example). This fact has a bearing upon discussions of "modern art" and may indicate that all controversies about "modernity," so far as they concern the artistic value, are idle talk. A work of modern art cannot be condemned because its pictorial structure does not conform to the perception of that uncomprehending beholder who sees in the deviation from natural appearances only distortion and artistic poverty. It becomes artistically worthless only if it is the stylized result of fixed rules externally taken over from modern art trends, since any pictorial work that is a product of a predetermined formula does not, of course, have its origin in a self-experienced, autonomous artistic process. On the other hand, one cannot fairly belittle a pictorial work merely because it closely approaches nature, but only when its apparent resemblance to the visible world is the result of imitation. Essentially a work of art is neither modern nor old, because it is always one and the same thing—the pictorial realization of that particular mental performance which is called visual conceiving.

As an assistance toward a clear understanding of the laws underlying the growth of inherent artistic abilities, this condensed presentation is, admittedly, idealized; in the actual evolutionary course of artistic abilities there are manifold variations and often complicated stages of transition. Furthermore, this presentation does not pretend to solve the entire problem of visual art. It is intended solely to explain basic pictorial artistic facts, ignoring all viewpoints from which a work of art is considered as a psychological, historical, or cultural document. The purpose of this entire study is to define that specific mental activity by which a work of art comes into existence. The theory expounded indicates that in the entire field of visual art, irrespective of whether it be fine or applied art, or architecture, the same mental process, the same kind of visual conceiving of qualitative relationships of form, is the decisive element. Always, in a work of art, visual cognition that is symbolized by a definite relationship of form is attained.

The theory presented in this book stresses the primary importance of the unadulterated creative process. Not the separate teaching of artistic elements of form according to the atomistic methods, not a special technique employed in a special medium, neither drawing, painting, sculpture, nor fine or applied art, is the final aim of the kind of art education here proposed. The goal is rather the natural cultivation of growing mental powers as they operate simultaneously and interfunctionally within the process of artistic configuration. All different media and techniques are subordinated to this purpose; and hence it may be necessary, in the artistic development of any given person, to encourage him to utilize many different materials, each of which will help him in realizing his particular stage of visual conceiving. It is in this way that an integral connection between man and his artistic achievement is established.

With the growing ability of visual conceiving, the work to be achieved grows also, within its structure, organically, stage by stage, from simple to more complex organizations of form. As each phase of development matures, it prepares thoroughly the ground for the manifestation of the next phase; that is, the principle of natural growth underlies the entire pedagogical procedure. As the main trend of this art education is inwardly determined by the law of man's growth of visual conception, and as the artistic result is the fruit of that growth, education (the natural cultivation of growing mental powers) and artistic activity (the pictorial realization of visual conception) become functionally united.

Within the course of artistic development as just described, each execution of a definite stroke, each touch of color, each bit of modeling the functional meaning of which within the structural order is thoroughly determined by the stage of visual conception, requires a high degree of motor control. Modern biology substantiates the belief that a change in any part of the human organism has a reflection upon the rest of the organism, and that "the average stage of tension of the single muscle is not determined by the muscle alone, but by the situation of the whole of the organism."[6] Thus it becomes comprehensible that in the evolution of innate artistic abilities man functions mentally and physically as a psychobiological whole. The unfolding of his

---

[6] Goldstein, *Human Nature*, p. 124.

artistic creativeness is intimately related to his whole being. Education, artistic activity, and the physical organism of man constitute a dynamic synthesis.

It seems obvious that the creation of the artistic form is attuned to a specific mental state of the creator. In other words, as there is an interconnection between the formative processes and the psychophysical responses of the originator, it can be said that he who forms artistically, in turn forms himself. Hence the unfolding of inherent art abilities takes on high significance with respect to the needs of the whole personality. This is especially true for those who suffer from a lack of self-confidence resulting from general neglect of their creative potentialities. It may further concern all those who live under depressive conditions, those who are occupied with automatic, mechanical work, who do not know the power that springs from the achievement of creation. All these fail to balance their personalities. Man becomes integrated by putting all his capacities into forceful interaction. In artistic activity, which is based upon the development of man's visual conceiving, the personality as a whole is constantly in play. All mental and physical energies act in balanced coördination.

Furthermore, since each artistically formed thing reveals the order and balance that its maker has given it, we may also say that things artistically created have a formative effect upon their surroundings. In a community in which the unfolding of innate artistic abilities becomes a general educational factor, and in which the balanced personality, the whole man and not the specialist, is the aim, the formative values within artistic processes may become of fundamental importance. The effect that genuine artistic work may have upon man, his production, his thinking, his feeling, makes a general unfolding of his art abilities an indispensable cultural element. It has always been a driving force in the creation of unified cultures. To bring forth such a culture becomes a vital necessity in a world that hitherto has been built far too much upon predetermined ideologies, a world in which everything except the essential nature of man seems so often to determine his environment. Artistic activity as the pictorial realization of man's visual conception may help to form a better world, more congenial to his nature.

The theory set forth in this chapter has full validity only if it can be applied equally to persons of different ages and of different mental and economic levels, and if it can be brought into general teaching practice. It has been shown that a child's spontaneous drawings not yet distorted by methods of teaching or imitation of nature possess intrinsically the artistic form, even though in a modest way. If one takes into consideration that the child grasps the world preponderantly by means of perceptual experience, then the creation of unity of form is his way of reaching visual cognition. His modest artistic activity thus becomes indispensable to his mental growth. All normal children display this inner drive for pictorial creation. Drawings on walls, doors, pavements, are visible proofs of the child's inborn creativeness. But because, in the course of general education, attention is still mainly directed toward acquisition of conceptual knowledge, the child's spontaneous drive for genuine visual cognition is neglected. As he grows older, the creative urge diminishes. It is therefore understandable that in most persons visual conception and its pictorial realization are not developed beyond the stages of childhood. But the ability itself has not vanished. It is always latent and can be awakened. A revival of inherent artistic abilities can only start, however, from the individual's stage of visual conception. For the educator it is a necessary prerequisite to obtain a thorough knowledge of these stages in order to be able to judge the work of his students objectively and to stimulate their organic artistic growth.

In order to prove the validity of the theory here presented, the following chapters demonstrate experiments with persons, from twelve to fifty-four years of age, who present wide variations in mental ability and in their educational, economic, and social backgrounds. Professional and business people, refugees, institutionalized delinquents, and mental defectives, are included.

The following case studies are mainly concerned with the unfolding of organized energies in the artistic process and its effect upon personality development, rather than with an interpretation of artistic activity as an expression of emotional factors, physical and psychological disturbances, and the like. Furthermore, it should be noted that the emphasis of these studies is not on differences between the various groups and individuals, although unquestionably those differences exist, but rather on certain fundamental laws of mental and specifically artistic growth which can be shown to apply universally. The present widespread tendency to focus atomistically on distinctions between subgroups may blind one's vision toward basic attributes of human nature, in comparison with which the individual variations are of secondary importance.

Report of the Experiment

The importance which attaches to the natural growth of a work of art can hardly be overestimated. All that is good and true in art depends on it. Art can flourish only when the artist follows the natural paths of production. Let him, then, get his result, however modest, by natural means, rather than strive to achieve something more brilliant, the outcome of a greater ability than he possesses; for such a work, being one of false pretense, must inevitably be condemned to the fate of all shams.

ADOLF HILDEBRAND

Chapter Three

THE EXPERIMENT WITH MENTAL DEFECTIVES

THE EXPERIMENT with mentally defective persons was carried out at the Southbury Training School, Southbury, Connecticut, a modern public institution for the care and education of mental defectives. Two courses were established, one for boys and the other for girls. The first group consisted of five boys and young men. Their ages ranged from eleven to twenty-nine and their I.Q.'s from 54 to 79. The second group consisted of five women (one of whom was dropped because she was often ill). Their ages ranged from twenty-one to thirty-five, and their I.Q.'s from 49 to 76. Both groups met one school day weekly for fifteen months. The participants represented the various levels of mental defectives with whom it seemed possible to work, from imbecile-moron to dull-normal levels.

The development of Selma, who had the lowest I.Q. of all the participants, will be described here to demonstrate the experiment.

Selma was a woman thirty years old with a mental age of six years and ten months. She had an I.Q. of 49, which means that she was on the borderline between imbecile and moron. She had never attended regular school. At the time of her admission to an institution for mental defectives she had only attended special classes. She showed little inclination to learn and was reported by her teachers to be "lazy and indifferent." At the time of her entrance into the Southbury Training School she was "unresponsive, inarticulate, and phlegmatic. She was sloppy, fat, unattractive in appearance, and had a vague empty stare. Her response to all questions consisted of a shake of her head or a groan. She would obey a direct command, she never caused any trouble or disturbance, but she showed absolutely no initiative in making friends or social contacts. She would prefer to withdraw to the fringe of a crowd and be a spectator and never a participant in cottage activities."

When the writer met her for the first time, she gave an impression of being very shy. It was difficult to have a conversation with her because she answered reluctantly and in monosyllables. When unoccupied, she seemed very restless and unhappy, and would walk through the workshop talking to herself. Now,

18. Drawing by a seven-year-old child.

in order to determine a person's stage of visual conception, the author generally asks him to draw whatever he wishes. From a person of Selma's mental level any spontaneous creative activity could hardly be expected. For this reason she was not requested to draw something of her own choice. Furthermore, it would have been impossible for her to respond to a sudden request that demanded quick decision; in fact, had she thus been called upon, it might have endangered her emotional equilibrium. In order to stimulate her, the author showed her a drawing done by a seven-year-old child, since it could be expected that her stage of development of visual conception would correspond to that of a normal child of approximately the same mental age as her own. It would seem reasonable to suppose that she could only grasp others' pictures that were in conformity with the stage of visual conception which she had already reached. Obviously she was able to react to the clear-cut, outlined picture shown her, since she found it "very pretty." (Picture 18.) After she had observed it for about ten minutes, it was removed and she was asked to make something similar in her own way. She was given a piece of paper 10 by 14 inches in size and an oil crayon. She started to work immediately and finished her drawing in twenty minutes.

19. Selma's first drawing, done with colored crayon.

—— When she was requested to show her work, her feelings of inferiority, her shyness, and even a certain anxiety gripped her. Turning her face away, she submitted her drawing with trembling hands. She obviously feared attention and criticism.

Her picture represents trees and flowers, with air, sky, and sun above. (Picture 19.) It has a subject similar to that of the drawing shown her, because trees and flowers are also the main content of that drawing. Furthermore, the structural order is almost the same; each single object stands by itself and is determined in its vertical direction by a horizontal base line. The forms of the trees are also visualized, as in the sample picture, by variability of direction. But in spite of all these points of likeness, Selma's drawing is by no means a copy of the picture shown. The similarity exists in the stage of development of visual conception. The peculiarity in the forms of the trees, their parallel arrangement, the long, horizontal base line by which the whole drawing attains a clear order, bring out the difference in the individual application of this stage of development. Irrespective of how crude and simple the drawing may appear, it must be recognized as showing independence of visual conception.

Selma's first picture—according to her own statement, the only one she had ever done—already indicates that even a mentally deficient person can create in a modest degree an ordered pictorial whole.

It was astonishing that she was able to accomplish even so simple a pictorial result, and the writer praised her for her work. Her reserved attitude disappeared at once, and a big smile spread over her face; apparently, a word of encouragement was what she needed. Another fact was still more astonishing. While the writer was engaged in supervising the work of the other girls belonging to the same group, Selma took some drawing paper from the desk and started a new picture (picture 20). She repeated almost the same subject. She placed in the center a large tree surrounded by smaller trees, on a long, wavy base line. Parallel to the base line, another line forms the lower border of the sky, which is colored blue, and the sun is in the right-hand part of the sky. Except for a little more careful execution of her drawing, there is no further development in the organization of form. But two essential facts must be noted: the smaller trees show a different application of the stage of variability of direction of lines, a variation of form invented by herself; and furthermore, the fact that she drew this picture spontaneously indicated the possibility of an unfolding of energies that no one had expected.

When Selma was requested to show her new work, she again displayed shyness and anxiety. After being praised a second time, she hesitatingly spoke a glad "Thank you."

In the afternoon of the same day, Selma selected some colored oil crayons out of a box which was at her disposal. It took her some time to find her "right" colors. Finally she chose brown, green, red, blue, and yellow. She paid no attention to more differentiated colors, such as violet and orange; even when they were presented to her, she definitely refused them. Her attitude was by no means strange if one takes into consideration the fact that her stage of development of visual conceiving determined her entire mental functioning. Just as she conceived lines in a very simple relationship of variability of direction, in like manner she approached undifferentiated colors. To employ differentiated colors such as violet and orange required a higher degree of ability to conceive

20. Selma's second drawing.

visually than Selma possessed at that time. As she would not have been able to order these colors into an organized pictorial structure, an undigested application of them would have confused her. Her rejection thereby took on a protective character.

With the suggestion that she proceed slowly and carefully, Selma went to work. She spent almost an hour in the execution of her third drawing (picture

21). The picture again represents a familiar content. Three trees are placed on a wavy base line. The space between the lower edge of the sheet of paper and the base line is filled in with green; obviously, that color carries the meaning of hills. The lower edge forms the horizontal base for five large flowers colored a darker green. As in her second picture, the upper line marking the sky is drawn parallel to the base line. The distinct construction of the whole drawing

21. Selma's third drawing.

and the more careful execution reveal that Selma is able to achieve an accurate performance when she is really interested in her subject and when this performance is suited to the stage of her mental development; in other words, when she can fully grasp what she is doing. Under such conditions, her drive for visual clearness impels her to a clear pictorial realization which serves as an impetus for the development of new pictorial ideas. The result is to be seen in the formation of the trees. Whereas in the earlier drawings she differentiated the branches either by simple dots or strokes, she now applies both in a rhythmic order representing blossoms and leaves. Within this rhythmic order the various colors find their best application. They become an essential factor in the pictorial structure. Each tree now has different colors for its blossoms, whereby they are clearly distinguished from one another. The tree on the right side has red leaves and green blossoms, which indicates that for Selma color has primarily a structural function and is not used as a faithful reproduction of nature.

Selma's creative activity may appear to many observers as insignificant. But these tiny signs of creativeness become of great importance if they concern individuals who are usually thought of as creatively sterile. Although the results achieved will always, in terms of normal potentialities, remain comparatively modest, their effect upon the feeble-minded producer may be of decisive consequence.

From these small beginnings, Selma's ability to create increased little by little. Each new picture revealed some variations, if only small ones. For weeks she repeated the same subject matter—trees, flowers, and hills,—but all her drawings manifested a simple but definite organization of form as the result of formative processes. He who does not observe the small changes in these pictures may see in them a "marked tendency to automatism," or a pointless repetition. Even art educators uninterested in the earliest documentations of artistic activity may consider these repetitions as special signs of mental immaturity or even of mental poverty. But such evaluations neither explain this phenomenon nor do justice to the significance it has for the individual concerned. Repetition is also a characteristic of the pictorial activity of young children. They also often remain for a long time in the same stage of development of visual conception. They repeat their simple signs for men, ships, and other objects which fill their interest, until they have apprehended them visually. In other words, repetition occurs until they have achieved a clear visual conception of the objects and made them part of their mental possessions. People who are mentally deficient, of a mental age analogous to that of young children, show a similar development in the unfolding of their artistic abilities. They pass through the same stages of visual conception and remain in those stages until they have grasped in clearest visual form the objects they draw. Since their mental capacities are more limited, their mental development takes a much slower course. But in both young children and deficients there is manifested an elementary impulse toward the acquisition of a mental possession through the medium of visual experience. Possession, either material or mental, means security. Any sign of losing it brings on a state of insecurity and confusion. To increase security through increase of possession is a prime necessity of the normal individual. To cling to possession with abnormal rigidity in order to be secure and to avoid confusion is the attitude of the mentally deficient. It was, therefore, an inner compulsion that made Selma display such rigidity in the repetitions of her subject. However, as she little by little modified and even enriched the structural organization of her pictures by new differentiations of form, her repetitions showed some

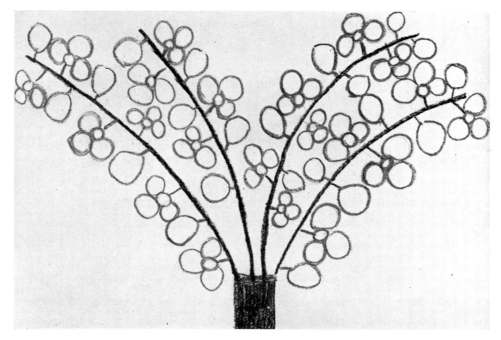

22. After almost three months, Selma worked out new shapes for blossoms and leaves.

signs of an increase in the acquisition of visual cognition. Repetition which contains within itself elements of change and development, irrespective of their minuteness, is formative activity. It was only through this step-by-step enrichment within the pictorial processes that Selma acquired the capacity of mastering a more complex creative configuration.

After weeks of such "repetitions," Selma still made the same dots and strokes for blossoms and leaves. One day, almost three months after her beginning the course, all her drawings were shown to her in the sequence of their production. The ensuing conversation brought Selma to a clearer observation of those dots and strokes for blossoms and leaves. When asked if she were able to draw these parts "better," she expressed signs of instant confusion.

She walked off, wandered through the workshop several times, and returned to say a shy "No." However, when she was advised to enlarge her trees on a larger sheet of paper so that she could see the single parts more clearly, she hesitatingly started to draw and tried to cover the whole sheet. But as she was used to another size of paper, she had to calculate visually the proportions of her new drawing. The problem placed her in extreme difficulties. Her struggle found an outlet in groans which indicated her desperate situation. She was so excited that her breath came shorter and faster. Yet she did not stop in her attempt. She tried it over and over again until she could organize her new drawing of a tree on the larger sheet of paper.

Selma's vigorous endeavor to find "better" shapes for her blossoms and leaves resulted in the formation of new pictorial elements. (Picture 22.) The simple dots previously used to represent blossoms are now given the shape of circles. Three of them, carrying the meaning of petals, surround a central circle as the center of a blossom; within this new formation, Selma again applies her previous conception of form—a single round dot. As with the blossoms, so with the leaves; instead of single strokes, large circles determine their shape, also. This progress may seem unimportant. However, when present in a mental defective with a low I.Q., it must be recognized as a positive factor in the free unfolding of ordered energies.

In all her earlier pictures Selma creates a definite organization in the relationship of the objects to one another. Trees and flowers are attached to their ground, the horizontal base line, in a vertical way which is the greatest contrast of direction to the ground. By this device the entire drawing receives an ordered stability. In spite of the fact that some details, such as branches, show a more advanced relationship of variability of direction with respect to the trunks, as soon as Selma faces a greater complex of objects, she regresses to the preceding stage of visual conception—the relationship of the horizontal-vertical. It has already been pointed out that this regression to an earlier stage follows a natural law. (See picture 11.) It can be found in all epochs, in the pictorial activity of primitive tribes, of children, and in genuine folk art.

For the purpose of stimulating Selma to a greater application of her creative abilities, the idea of a large complex of objects was brought to her notice. She was asked if she had ever seen a pond. Raising her voice—a sign of interest — she said, "Do you mean a pond with fish?" To this she received the answer: "Yes. Let's make a picture of such a pond and put your trees around it." She welcomed the suggestion and went to work immediately. She made a small drawing of a rectangular pond and put the trees around it, each big tree accompanied on each side by a small tree. The outline of the pond became the hori-

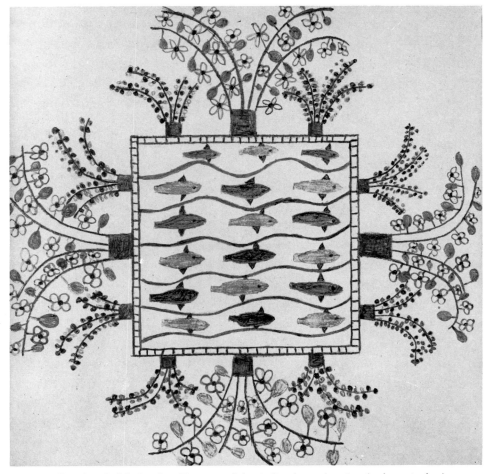

23. Pond with fish, bordered by trees. Selma's first large drawing (22 by 21 inches), done with colored crayons.

zontal base, and the trees were vertically directed from it all the way round. Selma intended to make the large trees with blossoms and leaves in accordance with her previous design, but as she could not carry out her ideas in this small space, a larger cardboard, 22 by 21 inches in size, was given her.

In carrying out her work on a larger scale (picture 23) she again met great difficulties. After she had completed the outline of the pond, she started to place the trees. Each time, she finished one tree perfectly but never calculated space for the next one. This lack of visualization of the whole placed her once more in a desperate situation. She had to do the work over several times. The nearer she came to a certain "perfection," the stronger became her desire for further progress. She proceeded, under constant admonition to work slowly. In drawing the contents of the pond she easily found her way. She divided the whole pond with blue wavy lines, representing waves, and between them she placed fish, alternately blue and red. It is interesting to note that the alternating color rhythm found in the blossoms and leaves previously drawn is applied in the pictorial realization of her fish. Again the same principle occurs: a visual cognition reached by the creation of a previous configuration of form is applied in the formation of another, similar, structural order.

The accomplishment of the larger color drawing substantiates the fact that Selma is well able to extend her modest creative ability to a certain degree. It is presupposed, of course, that the selection of her subject matter lies in the realm of her interest, and further, that the pictorial execution takes place in full conformity with her stage of development of visual conception.

Selma found a great deal of enjoyment in the completion of her picture, especially after having given herself so intensively to its accomplishment. Her own evaluation of her work was repeatedly expressed by: "Pretty, pretty."

The development of the other young women belonging to the same group was similar to Selma's. Their work had almost the same subject matter and reflected the same stage of development of visual conception. In their formative processes they faced the same "problem of form" and accomplished a similar structural organization. They were troubled more or less by the same difficulties. Together, they all went through the same experience and came to similar pictorial results. For this reason they were able to understand, appreciate, and enjoy their work interchangeably, as was often shown by their helping and advising one another. Each could contribute her abilities to the creation of a larger design.

Now, coöperation of this kind calls forth a common responsibility in all the co-workers of the group. Each one has not only to think of his own design, but also to watch the work of the others; because, without the right integration of each design into the whole structure, the unity of form of the larger design cannot be accomplished. The situation created, therefore, compels the participants to work with a flexible interchange of opinion concerning the pictorial construction of the whole.

Selma's color drawing of a pool surrounded by trees offered a good possibility for a large coöperative design by all four members of the group. It was discussed with them as a basis for a design to measure 30 by 40 inches. Selma had to draw her pool with waves and fish, first. As she wanted to make the lines "very good," she asked for the use of a yardstick. When it came to deter-

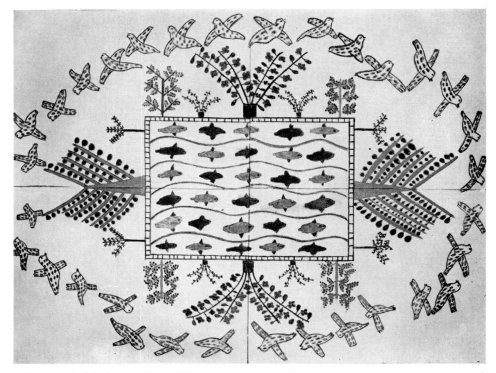

24. Pond with fish, bordered by different trees and with birds flying about. A coöperative work (30 by 40 inches) done in colored crayons by four mentally defective young women aged twenty, twenty-nine, thirty, and thirty-four.

mining the place for the pool, she again had difficulty; she could not seem to determine it by lines, but only to mark the place with her hands. All the girls discussed ways of solving this problem and finally worked it out so that Selma could draw the outlines. The first waves she drew came out to her full satisfaction, and as she drew the others in parallel relation to the first one, she went ahead unimpeded. (Picture 24.)

After Selma's part was done and the other girls praised her enthusiastically, she walked away very much embarrassed, obviously not accustomed to such an experience.

In the afternoon of the same day, all the girls had to select the places where they wanted to put their trees. One girl started by choosing places on the two long sides of the pool, following a simple, symmetrical order. Selma did exactly the same, selecting the other sides of the pool for her trees: a large one in the center, with blossoms, and an accompanying small tree on either side. While she was making her drawing she was much freer than before, and when she made some miscalculations in the placement of her trees she corrected her mistakes of her own accord. After Selma had finished her trees, she watched with eagle eye the two other girls who were still working. When one of them missed following the structure of the whole design, Selma was so excited that she pointed to the right place and wanted to draw the girl's tree herself. These other two girls had also selected places which were symmetrically ordered with relation to the other trees. When the girls had accomplished what they set out to do, there were still some empty spaces around their design. The girl who had drawn flying birds around her trees, in her previous pictures, carried out the suggestion of filling in the empty spaces around the large trees with her birds.

It is rare that mental defectives participate in a coöperative work which requires a mental concentration such as was necessary for the accomplishment of this large design. But these girls worked harmoniously together for more than three weeks. It must be emphasized again that this was only possible because each of them had arrived at the same stage of development of visual conception and because there existed a community of interest in the subject. As a result, they had an understanding of one another's work and were able, furthermore, to judge that work both in relation to their own and in relation to the whole order of the design. It is therefore understandable that a sense of responsibility arose in all of them—a responsibility to each other as well as to the success of the entire work. Selma, who because she usually worked very fast lost control and made mistakes, was forced to work slowly. Having to check herself for the sake of the success of the whole design was often very hard for her and went against her temperament. She, as well as the other girls, had to experience the feeling that her personal freedom had definite restrictions and that she was part of a small community in which each one had to contribute a share for the good of the whole.

The finished work was celebrated by a small party. Sitting in front of the large design, the girls regarded their achievement. A broad smile spread over

Selma's face: she knew that it was out of her drawing that this picture had emerged. She gained accordingly in a feeling of importance.

The next coöperative work was determined by another girl's color drawing of two crossing streets bordered on both sides by trees (picture 25). Selma contributed her designs of trees in the same manner as in the previous coöp-

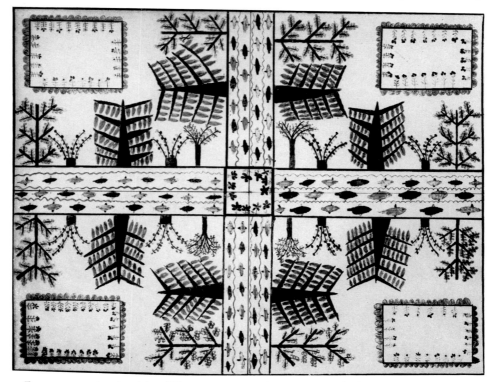

25. Four streams, bordered by different trees, meeting at a central island. A coöperative work (30 by 40 inches) done in colored crayons by five mentally defective young women aged twenty, twenty-four, twenty-nine, thirty, and thirty-four.

erative work. After the trees were completed, the girls began to discuss how to represent the streets. What objects should be drawn which would most clearly indicate a street? None of the girls knew what to do: no one of them could think of a way to solve the problem. Finally, Selma suggested, "Why don't we put fish in?" She meant, of course, to use the streets as streams. As the other girls liked Selma's design very much, they immediately agreed with this suggestion. In order to avoid later difficulties in execution, Selma was advised to draw the two streams alone on a separate sheet of paper. She worked by herself in a corner of the workshop. After a while, her well-known groan-

ing again signified that she was in trouble. Reluctantly she submitted a
color drawing and pointed to the center, where the streams met and crossed.
Because of the overlappings of the wave lines and the fishes she became so
confused that she was helpless. When she was asked what she thought could
be done with such a space, she decided to make a new drawing and leave the
space open. But again she did not attain full satisfaction. While the other girls
offered some suggestions which did not correspond with the subject matter
of this particular part, Selma concluded to "put sand into the water." She
started a new drawing, and when she came to the part that required a decision,
she filled the troublesome area with many brown spots. Continuing in this
way, she finally outlined the mass of spots, saying, "I make an island." In the
large design, she first drew the outline of her island by extending the outlines
of the streams. Then, in accordance with her previous order of trees, she used
the inside of the outline of her island as the base line for flowers.

In general, mentally deficient persons have a short span of attention and a
lack of concentration which causes their ideas to be fleeting and scattered. Any
occupation which can in any way strengthen these capacities is of decisive
educational importance. This does not mean that any mechanical manipulation which forces these patients into attention and concentration on their
work will be of therapeutic value. Just the contrary may occur: the patient
may attain control over his hands, he may even learn perfect manipulation of
a tool, he may become so used to this occupation that he is able to execute it
without personality participation in it, he may even feel at ease in doing it, but
the compulsory attention and concentration repeated over and over will throw
him into a mental and emotional rigidity worse than before. He may become
more or less adept at making things, but his personal relationship to them
remains external because the work does not have its origin within him; it does
not reflect himself. The performance is not related to the nature of his organism as a whole, as a psychobiological unity. Merely manual execution
employs only a very small fraction of the total organism, and the attention and
concentration it demands are not a result of the patient's inner decision. Only
when the innermost core of interest voluntarily determines the applying of
one's energies, when one feels that the work being done is an indivisible part
of oneself (a condition which requires, of course, that it be in full conformity
with one's own stage of visual conception), and when one is aware that attention and concentration are indispensable in order to realize oneself—only then

does work become constructive. It was this point of view which determined the selection of the next, and more extended, theme given to Selma.

In recognition of her contribution to the previous large designs, Selma was charged with the task of making a design for a tablecloth 20 by 30 inches in size, to be bordered on all sides by figures of her choice. Again she selected her favorite objects, trees and flowers, to which she added birds. From the

26. Selma concentrated all her efforts for weeks on this tablecloth (20 by 30 inches) designed and embroidered by herself.

beginning, she showed great interest in this task. Working almost without interruption, she completed her design in one school day of six hours. The following week the drawing was transferred to linen, and Selma started to embroider, which she knew how to do in a simple way. She selected the color of the thread herself. This work (picture 26) occupied her for several weeks, and during this time she became so absorbed in her task that nothing could disturb her. In the entire design, trees, flowers, and birds are clearly distinguished from one another; each figure is distinctly set off from its surrounding ground, but all are vertically directed to a horizontal base line determined by the four borders. All parts of this design together constitute a unified organization of form in which no part can be changed without changing the other parts. It may seem obvious that an activity such as this requires the utmost application of self. For a full and just evaluation of her work, it must be noted that it has its origin in Selma's stage of visual conception and that it has been accomplished without any outside help. Attention and concentration were the consequence of her intense interest in her work. The same attitude was evident in her production of two hooked rugs which she also designed and executed (pictures 27 and 28).

One day, while the other girls of this group were still occupied in carrying out their contribution to another large design, Selma seemed to become less interested in the activity of her co-workers. She even showed signs of growing uneasy. After a while she went to the desk, took some paper and colored crayons, and started spontaneously to make a new drawing, using again—with some minor additions—her special objects. Having accomplished a few simple designs revealing a perfect order and balance of form, she expressed a happy attitude seldom seen in her before. Each week thereafter, her spontaneous activity increased, and with it passionate enjoyment in her work.

After seven months of participation in the course, Selma had progressed so far that she was able to work independently. Usually, as soon as she entered the workshop she took some drawing paper and colored crayons and started to work spontaneously. Her pictures were still of her trees, the smaller ones with dots and strokes, the large ones with different kinds of blossoms; also still evident were flowers, dogs, bluebirds, fish, waves of water, and hills. In the next two months Selma produced thirty complete designs, each different from the others, four of which are here reproduced (pictures 29, 30, 31, 32). Not only did she display an extraordinary variety of objects, but the form of those objects in which she was most interested, such as trees, revealed a greater differentiation of her stage of visual conception. In the further course of her spontaneous activity she developed a mental attitude characterized by constant observation and control of the effect of each single form upon the next one. This formative process of creating a lawfully constructed order was so pronounced that it gave the impression of springing from a desire to master the entire design.

This unique kind of production by a person whose mental level is marked by a low I.Q. reveals a definite kind of intelligence which hitherto has not been appreciated or discovered by any of the standard intelligence tests in

27 (above) and 28 (below). Selma's two hooked rugs, designed and
executed by herself. (Each, 25 by 32 inches.)

use. Nevertheless, it must be considered as intelligence, "because perception of relationship between what is done and what is undergone constitutes the work of intelligence, and because the artist is controlled in the process of his work by his grasp of the connection between what he has already done and what he is to do next. . . . Moreover, he has to see each particular connection of doing and undergoing in relation to the whole that he desires to produce. To apprehend such relations is to think, and is one of the most exacting modes of thought."[1] Constant observation, and that type of intelligence which is exercised in perceiving form relationships, were employed by Selma in order to accomplish her thirty designs.

Each of these color drawings reveals a definite order and a lawful organization by which they attain a perfect unity of form. It may seem obvious that inner mental and emotional balance and order underlie the creation of such synthesis of form. And, as has already been indicated in the statement of the theory sustaining this experiment, there is an interrelationship between the formative processes and the mental and emotional state of the individual who creates such order of form. It can therefore be said that he who forms something artistically, in turn forms himself. This assertion may become the more clearly understandable if one considers the human being as a functional unity in terms of a psychobiological whole. A change grounded in so basic a mental activity as the organic unfolding and development of visual conceiving and its pictorial realization will in turn cause changes in the entire organism. The functional unity becomes clear when one takes into account the behavioral components which go to make up artistic activity as discussed in the preceding paragraphs.

Selma's major sphere of interest became more and more centered in her work. By her choosing her colors, her enjoying the harmony of color-and-line combination and, finally, the organized picture as a visually comprehensible totality, her emotional life became more overtly expressed than ever before. By constant control of the interrelationship of all pictorial elements and their mutually dependent effects her visual thinking was developed. By deciding upon her themes and materials as well as independently correcting distorted unity of form she evolved directed conceptual thinking. Finally, her work caused a definite reorganization of her physical behavior. The tension of the particular arm muscle she used in her work affected the attitude of her entire

[1] John Dewey, *Art as Experience* (New York: Minton, Balch, 1934), p. 45.

29 and 30. Two of thirty designs by Selma.

31 and 32. Two of thirty designs by Selma.

body, as was seen most clearly when she assumed a complicated stance or position in the execution of a decisive line. All these factors operated in a constant interfunctional unity. They lose their significance as soon as they are separated from one another. They can only be understood and evaluated in their relation to the unified creative process and its effect upon the whole personality.

As she became more aware of her creative potentialities, Selma underwent a definite change, a change toward a "more formed personality." Prior to her participation in the course, it would have been impossible for her to carry out a commission outside the workshop, especially since she had a poor spatial orientation of the layout of the institution. She was obviously confused by the many different buildings and the many paths leading to them. It was difficult to persuade her to do errands which would require her going to other parts of the institution. Little by little, organized work that was in full conformity with her mental capacities, the exercise of a constant visual control, developed in her a visual orientation combined with clearness of thought. After nine months of her art activity, she was asked one day to go to the office of the psychologist in the administration building to call for a hooked rug which she herself had made. At first she hesitated and became embarrassed, but after repeated requests she reluctantly made up her mind, and when another girl offered to accompany her she rejected any help. This was the first time since her admission to the institution that Selma revealed such courage and determination in accomplishing an assignment outside of the workshop and her daily routine. Obviously encouraged by this experience, she two weeks later took over the responsibility of guiding another girl, who was unable to orient herself on the institution grounds, to the same office.

Before participating in the experimental group, Selma lived a barren existence filled only with daily routine work. The simple tasks she performed were the result of manipulations that had been drilled into her. They brought her neither interest nor stimulation. There seemed to be no place where she could fit into the life of the institution. Constantly indifferent, unable to establish any contact between her occupation and her needs, she developed a chronic apprehension and shyness that made her so restless and insecure that she avoided the smallest difficulties. After sixteen years of institutional life, this was her state. Through the opportunity of participating in the experimental group, a basic function of her mental existence to conceive and to grasp her own world by images, and even to realize them in a well-organized fashion, had been awakened and developed within her in conformity with her natural capacity. Through these processes, her entire interest, her feeling and thinking, her physical behavior, her personality as a whole, had been affected. At the beginning of her activity in the experimental group, Selma was indecisive and insecure about what to do with herself. She wandered helplessly through the studio. Seven months later, she started her work spontaneously; she had definite ideas about her pictorial themes; she was determined in the execution of her pictures as well as in the manipulation of her material. Little by little her former nervous impulsiveness was replaced by a controlled and quiet determination. If she made mistakes, such as spoiling the order of form, she changed her color drawing independently until she reëstablished the pictorial organization. All these spontaneous actions indicated an increased self-assurance and a gain in her inner security, through which she reached a greater amount of freedom. In the first few months of her activity in the course she was reserved, silent, and shy; she even avoided any kind of conversation. After nine months she frequently initiated conversations with her co-workers. She always looked forward impatiently to making new designs. In the course of her work she often enjoyed singing her favorite song, "There'll be blue birds over the white cliffs of Dover." Step by step with each new achievement, she built up her creative self, her self-realization. She attained results, she "mastered" situations. Selma felt her own worth. She seemed to be finding her niche, and that discovery gave her security. She showed characteristics of a normal and healthy human being. She overcame her instability which arose from her clash with the world, not by virtue "of anxiety, but through the joy of coming to terms with the world."

REPORT ON SELMA

The following report prepared by Dr. Seymour Sarason, chief psychologist of the Southbury Training School, who witnessed the entire experiment at Southbury, may throw light upon the psychological aspects of Selma's development.

"A problem that is of much psychological importance in this case is the relation between Selma's artistic activity and her personality development. What is there about the background of this girl that might help explain her surprising achievements in quality as well as in quantity? Is the marked change in her behavior the result of the specific activity to which she was exposed? Could a similar change be obtained from other kinds of activity?

— "The following is a brief abstract of the girl's case history:

"At the time of admission in 1927 to an institution for mentally defective children, Selma was living with her aunt. The father had died when she was ten, and the mother when she was twelve. At the age of three Selma had been burned over a large portion of her body, and extensive scars have remained. According to informants, the aunt frequently and severely maltreated the girl. She would hit her on the head, whip her unmercifully, and call her all kinds of names. The aunt frequently drank. At one time she dragged Selma by the hair and beat her. There is little known about Selma's parents except that both drank a good deal, also. The aunt wanted to get rid of Selma and was responsible for her institutionalization. After admission, Selma received only one visitor during the first five years, and in 1943 there is a record of another. Her institutional behavior was poor and she was considered quiet, deceitful, peculiar, and possibly hallucinated because she talked to herself and grimaced and smiled in a strange fashion. She was always assigned the most routine and simple tasks, which she would complete only under close supervision. In 1942 she was transferred to the Southbury Training School.

"In view of such a background Selma's fearfulness, marked introversion, impulsiveness, and inefficiency became more understandable. Attention, affection, and sympathetic understanding were rarely, if ever, extended to her. Considered severely retarded and peculiar, it is not strange that she was given work which in no way served as an outlet for her ability or feelings. There was no realization that this girl could develop within her own limitations in any activity in an orderly and organized fashion.

"One might be tempted to explain the astonishing development in this girl's achievement and behavior simply by the change from a hostile environment to a friendly and humane one. Therefore, it must be pointed out that the progress described in this report occurred after sixteen years of institutional life and only when she had been given the opportunity of participating in the experimental group. For the first time this girl was presented with a task which she could do in her own way. She was not told how to do it and did not have to conform with the preconceived ideas of others. Her initial work was rewarded with praise which served as the impetus for further attempts. Each new work, in itself an indestructible gestaltformation, was a source of satisfaction to Selma. She was able to see for herself the growth in her drawings. A critical awareness became evident in her striving to correct her mistakes and to do better the next time. More and more of her attention and energies became focused on her work. Selma was accepted and praised by people for something which came from herself and was truly her 'own'. Her impulsiveness decreased; she became fastidious in the execution of her drawings; she became bolder in the scope of her work and able to identify herself with it."

"Concomitant with the development in the realm of visual conceiving was a striking change in Selma's institutional behavior. The growth of highly organized form evident in her pictorial work corresponds with Selma's development toward a more unified personality. She did not hide her head or run away when engaged in conversation. She would seek a person out and talk to him—something which she had never been observed to do. Even when visitors in the institution tried to talk to her, Selma would not manifest the panic or fear she formerly did. The girl seemed happier and more secure than ever before.

"It might be said that the change in Selma's behavior could be attributed to the fact that she was receiving praise and attention to an extent which never before had been given her. That praise and attention played a role cannot be denied. Such an interpretation, however, disregards the fact that there is in her work an observable orderly development of gestaltformation. What seems to be basic in this case is that this girl was given an opportunity to merge in one activity emotional satisfaction, full utilization of energies, planning and foresight, and well-configurated visual expression. It is the educational and therapeutic significance of the genuine artistic process that it embodies in an indivisible manner so many different aspects of human functioning.

"The significance of Selma's case is that it demonstrates the importance of basic educational and therapeutical procedures on the individual's natural potentialities for organized development. To ask a person to reproduce, either from model or memory, a particular scene or object neglects the fact that such a task may well be foreign to the individual's interest and needs as well as beyond his particular level of visual conceiving. In such a case the discrepancy between task and result does not allow the individual to identify himself with what he has done; no opportunity has been given to 'grow into his work'. One might generalize and say that unless work stems from the natural growth of abilities it will have little effect on the personality.

"The opportunity to observe the application of this new approach with various groups at Southbury gave additional data which are of psychological and educational significance.

"The main experimental groups with whom the most time was spent were those of feeble-minded boys and girls. Each group met one day a week in a large, spacious workroom. Work began in the morning and continued until lunchtime, after which work was resumed and continued until four o'clock in the afternoon. The striking result observed in the behavior of these children was the increased interest with which they approached the class. This was most clear in their sustained manner of work. They did not approach the class as if it were a necessary chore, but with an enthusiasm which is not typical of defectives. It is not unusual to see defectives in training schools engaged for several hours in one task—such as weaving, rugmaking, basketry, and other activities found in occupational therapy units. Analysis of these tasks will reveal that in practically each case the child need possess no originality or demonstrate any creativity in order to do an acceptable job. The most important requisite demanded of the child is that he repeats monotonously a sequence of movements. In such a case imitation and persistence are the basic factors in performing a particular task. However, sustained activity is not obtained with defectives when the task involved is drawing, especially, as is usual, when drawing consists either of obvious imitation of complex forms in the environment or aims at mere emotional 'self-expression.' Even with normal children, sustained activity in drawing (when it consists of mere imitation or reproduction) is the exception rather than the rule. It was, therefore, surprising to observe how the children in the present experimental groups would work for relatively long periods of time, genuinely interested in what they were drawing. It should be remembered that these children were neither compelled to copy models nor simply left to themselves, but led to develop self-judgment of their work in accordance with their ability of visual comprehension.

"The finding as to increased activity and interest is corroborated not only by observation of each child working alone, but in the increased group feeling which developed as the class continued. At the beginning of the experiment each child worked alone, and it was only after several months that the children worked together on a theme of their own choosing. When working in a group, each member carefully watched the others so that nothing would be done to spoil the coöperative work. They would caution each other, admonish each other when laxity was evident, and in general displayed a high level of group responsibility. When one keeps in mind the fact that these children were in similar stages of development of visual conception and so 'understood more easily the work of the others', and that all derived a sense of pride from their work, it becomes clear how each member of the group was able to identify with the others. This level of social interaction is, to say the least, unusual among feeble-minded children. The fact that it was 'naturally' developed in this study suggests a profound change in one's orientation as to the education of the mentally deficient.

"One of the schoolteachers who utilized with her own class the same techniques and procedures as were employed with the experimental group presented this statement concerning the results she obtained.

" 'Before the new approach was introduced, three quarters of the children used to ask before they went to their daily art class, "Do we have to go to art?" The other quarter were not averse to going to art class, because of their success in copying objects or other pictures put before them and because of the admiration that followed from the less imitative pupils. Since the majority of the class derived no satisfaction from their art work, disciplinary problems ensued. Because of failures in art as a result of their inability to copy, the boys would resort to tracing pictures instead of completing their assigned work. Those that copied well were respected by the class. They were the best "drawers."

" 'Participation in a weekly seminar for teachers made it possible for me to apply in my classroom the theory underlying the work in the experimental group. Since time could not be allocated for art in the classroom, the boys were permitted to work on their drawings as seat work only when their individual academic lesson was completed. They usually drew something which was centered about a comprehensible theme and which was definitely within their restricted mental capacity. Each drawing seemed as unique as the child that conceived it. A name on a picture signifying the little artist was superfluous.

" 'The boys became more critical of their work. Disciplinary problems were alleviated. The most stimulating consequence was that their span of concentration became longer. They no longer daydreamed or displayed as frequent signs of instability as before. They did not show any desire to copy. For example, in the absence one day of the art instructor, a substitute took charge of the art class. Christmas cards were given to the boys to copy. They resented this but had to copy because they were instructed to do so. One boy copied a picture and claimed it to be his own idea. The rest of the class immediately embarrassed him by laughing at him and telling him that he was "too lazy to do his own work."

" 'The change in the children's behavior has been transferred from the classroom into their cottage life. At present they have "requisitions" from interested friends for their drawings which have been transferred from paper to unbleached muslin, colored with oil crayons, and pressed with a hot iron. This work is done in the evening at their respective cottages. When completed, the class as a whole judges the drawings before they are delivered to the prospective buyer. If satisfactory, they are released and the proceeds go into the boys' funds, upon which they may draw at any time.'[2]

"After the results of the children's work were displayed, a desire was expressed by some of the school employees for a workshop class to be held for them one night a week. It is of interest to note how the work of the children encouraged the employees, many of whom disliked drawing because of the 'mess that resulted', to express themselves pictorially. It would seem as if the drawings of the children, simple in appearance but organized totalities of form, were on a level of development which closely approximated the level of visual conception of the employees. In fact, the early drawings of these employees were similar in organization of form to those of the children.

"The development of some of the employees was indeed remarkable. In the initial class there was much mental groaning and wailing as the members of the group found it impossible to realize pictorially their ideas. In practically every case there was an obvious attempt to reproduce mechanically a scene so that it contained as many details as memory would allow. The discrepancy between intent and result was so noticeable as to make several of the group discouraged and disillusioned. As one of the members said, 'I can't make it look the way I want it to look—the way it should look'. The attitude that drawing consisted of pictorially reproducing details from memory was a hard one to dispel. It took some time before the members of the group experienced through their own work that it was impossible for their pictorial realization to contain the myriad of details found in nature, but that their aim should be to see in their drawing 'that which they want to see' in clear and lucid organization, no matter on how primitive a level one must begin.

---

[2] The writer wishes to thank Miss Florence Marcktell, special education teacher at the Southbury Training School, for this report.

"When these difficulties were overcome, several of the group showed surprising development to more differentiated artistic stages. In the case of two employees, neither of whom had ever attempted drawing as a recreational activity because they believed they were completely lacking artistic talent, personality changes of some depth were observed as they became aware of the growth in their works.

"The results obtained from the groups at Southbury emphasize a basic problem in psychology: the differentiation between capacity and functioning. Those who have worked closely with institutionalized mental defectives have been struck time and again by the discrepancy between intelligence-test scores and actual functioning. It is not rare to see so-called defectives do work which obviously requires a mental level that is higher than the individual's mental age or intelligence quotient. Such discrepancy is not a problem found only with defectives; clinical experience with nondefective individuals also leads one to the conclusion that there are many whose capacities are not in evidence in their day-to-day functioning. It is important, therefore, to see how results from another field, in this case visual art, corroborate clinical experience. The significance of the results from the Southbury groups (patients and employees) is that a clear picture is obtained of the discrepancy between potential capacity and actual functioning. The contrast between the initial efforts of the subjects and their final work shows how careful one must be in evaluating potentiality.

"To those who are in the field of the education of the feeble-minded, Professor Schaefer-Simmern's results at Southbury reveal a definite challenge: one can no longer regard the subnormal individual as lacking the capacity for organic growth of his limited mental abilities. It remains for those in special education to investigate the general principles underlying this experiment. Its implications applied to different activities may be richly rewarded for a better understanding of individual development."

⋄   ⋄   ⋄

The following pages show embroideries, printed fabrics, and designs cooperatively done by several girls or boys, which exemplify achievements of other members of the Southbury experiment. It must be noted that all students started from simple scribbles and proceeded to the stages of development shown in these illustrations (pictures 33 to 40).

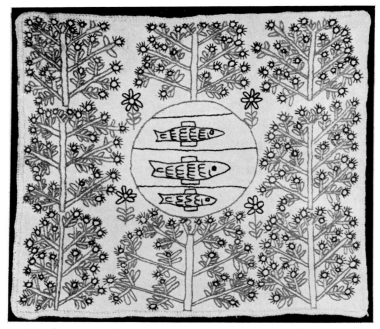

33. "Pool surrounded by blossoming trees" (13 by 14 inches), by a woman of thirty-four with an I.Q. of 67, after nine months in the course.

34. "Garden with bushes" (14 by 14 inches), by a woman of twenty-six with an I.Q. of 50, after eleven months in the course.

35. "Roosters between flowers and grass," an embroidery (13 by 14 inches) designed and executed by a young woman of thirty with an I.Q. of 76.

36. Appliqué (14 by 14 inches) done by the same young woman.

37. "Trees in blossom," design for a rug (40 by 30 inches) done in colored crayons by four mentally defective young women aged twenty, twenty-nine, thirty, and thirty-four. The upper two levels were done first and then repeated in reverse order. For the purpose of attaining an easy balance for the whole design, each level was started from the central tree and extended outward.

38. Printed fabric. This idea of a tree, clearly demonstrating the stage of variability of direction of lines, was designed, cut in linoleum, and printed on cloth by a young woman of thirty with an I.Q. of 76. The work shows how early stages of artistic activity have that intrinsic decorative quality which is indispensable for a genuine applied work of art.

39. "Paradise," colored drawing (40 by 30 inches) done as a coöperative work by five mentally defective boys and young men ranging in age from twelve to thirty years. A suggestion was given them of starting the entire design with the main theme, "Adam and Eve under the Tree." The boys selected the center of the working area (four pieces of cardboard joined in one) as the right place for this theme; and thus they established the clearest figure-ground relationship. The other objects were pictorially organized by following a simple order of parallelism in relation to the central design and to each other.

40. "Flower garden," a drawing made with oil crayons on a cotton sheet (40 by 30 inches), later pressed with a hot iron; a coöperative work done by five feeble-minded boys aged eleven, twelve, thirteen, and fourteen years. Before drawing the flowers on cloth, each boy prepared his own flower thoroughly on a sheet of paper. Each level was started from the central design and extended outward.

Chapter Four

THE EXPERIMENT
WITH DELINQUENTS

THE EXPERIMENT with delinquents, extending from March, 1940, to September, 1942, was carried out at the New York City Reformatory, in New Hampton, New York. Eighteen boys participated in the course, six of whom remained for only a few lessons because they were either paroled or transferred from the institution. There were seven boys who participated for five months, and five boys for seven months. Their ages ranged from seventeen to twenty-two and their I.Q.'s from 72 to 107. Although the participants represented various mental and educational levels, most of them were low in intelligence. The group met one and one-half days each week.

The development of Michael, who belonged to the lower intelligence level and who remained in the course for seven months, is chosen to demonstrate the experiment.

Michael was twenty years of age, a first-generation American of Greek descent, in religion a Catholic. He had a very limited educational background, having attended school only to the third grade because of illness. In a state school, which he attended for a short time, he gained some knowledge of carpentry. After this he helped his mother, who worked as a superintendent of two buildings in New York City. The psychological report describes him as "an immature youth who has developed deep feelings of inferiority due largely to little mingling with people and poor educational background. He is lacking in confidence, both in himself and socially. . . . He is quite unable to handle himself among more aggressive boys. . . . He is very passive and timid. . . . His intelligence quotient is 76, which places him near the borderline of mental defective."

Michael at first appeared quiet and reserved. He seemed depressed, but was friendly. He did not display interest and seemed rather indifferent to the work.

At the suggestion that he draw whatever he liked, he made a clumsy animal which could have been done by a child of about eight years of age (picture 41). Asked what his drawing represented, he replied: "A horse. I always like to be near horses. When I see one, I walk up to it and pet it. I have a natural feeling for horses just like I have for dogs." Referring to his picture, he said: "But I don't like it. It's no good." Michael was not asked why he

41. Michael's first drawing.

did not like his drawing, for then he would have had to explain it in verbal terms, that is, abstractly. Since this might have hindered him from judging his picture visually, he was simply given the suggestion of drawing, in accordance with his own ideas, a "better horse." The term "better" did not influence him, for it left him free to apply it as he wished.

Michael's first drawing, clumsy as it may appear, already contains substantial elements of an organized pictorial structure. It shows his horse as a total object: the whole body, four legs, tail, and ears have been visualized. The whole form of his horse is realized as an outlined intentional figure, extended and directed according to the beginning stage of variability of direction. Except for the jaw line, which partly covers the neck, no part interferes with another. Furthermore, the front legs as well as the hind ones tend to be in a relationship of direction to one another. The drawing, undeveloped as it may be, must therefore be considered the result of a simple visual comprehension of the object and not an imitation of an arbitrary aspect of a horse.

Michael was asked to observe his drawing for a while, which he did; and then he said, "I don't like it at all." This is a natural reaction for a twenty-year-old whose conceptual knowledge of a horse is much more developed than his visual conception of it. Nevertheless, he was stimulated to try again.

42. Michael's second drawing. He was advised to fill in the penciled outline with black ink. The silhouette, creating a better figure-ground relationship, facilitated his visual judgment of the entire drawing.

The second drawing (picture 42) represents a larger theme: "Horse standing on grass beside a wooden fence." The fact that Michael spontaneously chose a larger theme indicates a greater interest in his work. In order that he might judge his drawing better, he was advised to fill in his pencil drawing with black ink. The resulting silhouette, a black spot with a white surrounding area, gave him a better opportunity to criticize his drawing visually than the penciled outline. After observing his drawing for a while, Michael remarked: "The legs look like a dog's legs. In my next picture I'm going to try to make them look like a horse's legs."

In spite of its awkwardness, this drawing shows on close observation that there are already some improvements. They consist not in an increase of imitative faithfulness, but in a clarification of the pictorial form for the sake of better visual comprehension. It is for this purpose that the body is simplified to an approximately rectangular form to which the legs are attached singly and distinctly. The neck, clearly separated from the body, attains its proper shape and is related to the head also as a rectangle. In the previous picture, the upper parts of the hind legs are not clearly visualized. Now they are distinctly separated, with the legs of each pair in a definite relationship of direction to each other. Even the tail, which in the previous drawing was arbitrarily

43. Michael's third drawing.

extended from the body, is now given a definite place, which is determined by the upper right-hand edge of the rectangular body. By these means the drawing achieves a clearer structural order and becomes more easily grasped visually.

Michael's third drawing of a horse (picture 43) displays a still greater simplification and even a certain stiffness of expression, especially since the legs are no longer bent. He obviously regressed to an earlier stage of visual conceiving—the stage of the greatest contrast of direction—in order to attain a clearer idea of his object. He applies the same principle to the relationship between the grass and the ground. But the formation of each leg already indicates a distinction between upper and lower leg, determined by the presence—for the first time—of the knee. Michael's interest in his work must have again increased, because he added to the contents of his drawing another new object, a tree. The structural order of the tree indicates the beginning of a variability of direction of lines, as is to be seen in the formation of the trunk and in the relationship between the branches and the trunk as well as between the branches separately. The slanting outlines of the horse's legs had

44. Michael's fourth drawing.

already appeared in the previous drawings. The entire picture, therefore, represents a clear type of stage of transition from greatest contrast of direction to variability of direction of lines.

Michael was obviously aware of his progress. With a determination he had not expressed before, he said, "Next week I will make it still better."

His fourth picture marks a decisive step in his development. (Picture 44.) In his third drawing he just started to conceive the tree according to the stage of variability of direction of lines; in this one he applies his conception of form in a relatively complicated fashion and in a unity of direction to the whole tree. The application of the same principle appears also in the new shape of the grass. Even the change in the figure of the horse can be explained only by the fact that Michael put into practice his newly attained comprehension of form. As a result, the outlines of the neck, the lower line of the body, and the new shapes of the legs give to the whole figure a slight increase of tension and vitality. In sum, the unified structure of the whole picture was determined by the application of a new conception of form which was conditioned by an earlier one and which grew organically from it. The unity of this simple pictorial organization is, therefore, the outcome of an independent mental activity, the process of visual conceiving.

The changes in these four drawings manifest an unfolding of Michael's creative abilities which could hardly have been expected. This unfolding shows how little is known of a person's mental potentialities, and furthermore, how such potentialities can be brought out. It should be emphasized that the only instruction given consisted of the following advice: to work as slowly as possible; after completing the drawing, to observe it at length; if the outline was not clear enough, to fill it in with black ink to make a silhouette; and whenever a change seemed necessary, to start a new drawing. Michael was aware that he had made his pictures by hard concentration, and definitely felt that he had done the work himself. After finishing his fourth drawing, he wrote on the reverse side of the paper: "I improved this last picture so much I can not believe that I really done it and I am going to try to make a whole herd of horses and colts by their mothers and a king horse on a nearby hill." Michael's own statement reveals that an "immature youth . . . lacking in confidence" is gaining new faith in himself.

A week later Michael went to work as soon as he entered the workshop; but he did not pursue his idea of a herd of horses. He started three new drawings, and then destroyed them. Finally, in the late afternoon, he finished his picture. (Picture 45.) The relatively complicated form of the tree at the right-hand side of the drawing may indicate the struggle he had in accomplishing this pictorial formation. It reveals a further application of the previous conception of form. Using in a more extended way the same angles by which he had related larger and smaller branches to one another, he achieved greater complexity within the organization of the whole structure. The same construction of form is found in the newly added bush at the left-hand side, with the difference that this object is not so complicated as the tree. However, it obtains a vigorous clearness of form. Each detail is placed in so orderly a fashion that it seems impossible to undertake a single change without destroying the whole pictorial configuration.

In Michael's earlier pictures almost all objects and their parts appear singly, without interference with one another. Where such interferences do occur, they are soon corrected.[1] Each figure is distinctly set off from its environment by the light surrounding ground. In other words, figure and light ground are in a definite relationship to each other, the one bringing out the other; the out-

45. After four weeks of participation in the course, Michael reached the stage at which he realized for the first time the overlapping of limbs.

lined objects always carry figural meaning. In the earlier pictures the horse is drawn in such a way that all four legs appear singly as downward extensions of the body. (The silhouettes do not indicate this as clearly as picture 41.) In the formation of the horse in picture 45 a change occurs. The legs nearer the observer are no longer a downward extension, but partly cover the body as well as the upper parts of the legs farther from the observer. Just as all parts of this drawing are distinctly outlined against their light ground, so the legs on the near side are outlined as independent, single objects against the

---

[1] In picture 43 the tree interferes with the fence; in picture 44 the tree is clearly separated from the fence. In the formation of the fence the overlapping is a necessary feature characteristic of the object itself; otherwise it would not represent a fence. Quite different is the representation of the legs of an animal in relation to the body, or of the tree in relation to the fence. Here, overlappings are not essential and are therefore avoided.

body and the upper parts of the far-side legs. Thus, the legs nearer the observer take on the characteristic of figure against a new ground, namely, the surrounding body and the upper parts of the farther legs. In other words, the relationship of figure and ground between all outlined objects and their light surrounding is now applied to the relationship between the near-side legs and the upper part of the far-side legs and the lower body, which assume the pictorial function of ground meaning to the near-side legs.

This change in the pictorial structure is based upon the same principle as has been noted of previous changes in Michael's work: a relationship of form that has already been accomplished in parts of a picture is, in turn, applied to the rest of the picture.

The representation of the near-side legs as single, outlined figures marks a stage of transition toward a further relationship of form, namely, the stage of borderless transition from parts with figural meaning to parts with ground meaning. By means of this transition the effect of overlapping is attained and with it a new idea of spatial depth.

Such overlapping has already been discussed, but in order to clarify an understanding of its function in a different pictorial application, and for the sake of throwing light on Michael's progress of visual conceiving, it will now be discussed again.

It has been shown that the near-side legs, which are entirely bordered by their outlines, carry figural meaning. A close observation reveals that the far-side legs are only outlined by their own contour against the light surrounding ground. The upper parts of the far-side legs, which do not have their own contours but are bordered by the outlines of the lower part of the body and the upper parts of the near-side legs, attain ground meaning with respect to these neighboring objects. This means that the far-side legs contain both figural meaning and ground meaning. Their outlined areas with figural meaning pass gradually over, by loss of their own contour, into areas that have the pictorial function of ground with reference to their adjacent parts. This pictorial function through which one part brings out distinctly its neighboring part is the result of a new way of visual conceiving which in turn leads to a new idea of spatial depth. It seems obvious that this process of conceiving is a creative one, the result of which cannot be duplicated by either imitation or reproduction, and that it points to Michael's spontaneously increased ability in visual organization.

Michael's interest in his work was best expressed when he entered the workshop a week later. "All this week I have thought about my horse. I know what I'm going to do." Surprisingly, he selected a much larger sheet of paper (30 by 40 inches) and started to draw a new picture of a horse. Since he had difficulties in handling this sheet of paper on the workbench, he decided to

46. By means of greater application of the principle of variability of lines, more tension in the entire figure of the horse was attained.

build an easel. The enlargement of his drawing presented difficulties, but he did not give up and displayed a perseverance he had never shown before. He had to draw his theme over and over again. After having done five pictures which were not to his satisfaction, he finally succeeded. (Picture 46.) He observed his drawing for a long time, as he was constantly advised to do, and then decided to fill in the entire picture with brown color in order to make a brown horse. In order to distinguish the legs from the body, he drew the overlappings in white. The drawing represents a horse, its right foreleg lifted, standing on a ground with grass and a bush in front of it.

The first impression of this drawing is an impression of much greater tension throughout the entire figure. The tension can only be attributed to the fact that Michael applied his stage of visual conception—that is, the relationship of variability of direction—to the entire figure in a much higher degree than in his earlier pictures. Even the movement in the right front leg can only be explained by this fact. But note the change in the legs nearest the observer in relation to the body. Their outlines, which still carry figural meaning against the body, which represents ground meaning, are no longer closed. They are open at the top. This means a further application of the stage of borderless transition, the figural meaning of the outlined areas of these legs going over, borderless, into areas of the body which carry ground meaning. The horse is now visually conceived as a new, coherent, intentional figure on a more differentiated stage of visual conceiving.

The fact that this comparatively complicated pictorial configuration is attained by Michael's spontaneous ability to conceive visually new relationships of form, so that one form emerges out of the preceding one, points clearly to the organic development of his creative abilities.

The discovery that he was able to perform unexpected tasks gave Michael new courage. He saw other boys of the same experimental group cutting their designs in linoleum and printing them on cloth for window curtains to be used in a new building at the institution. He felt that he could do the same thing, using his design of a horse, bush, and grass. The size of the curtain was measured, to determine whether the design of a single horse with bush and grass could be repeated crosswise. Michael considered the problem a moment, and said: "Why not use trees and bushes? I know how to make a tree." But when he tried his design on paper the size of the window curtain, using the rhythm of large tree, horse with bush, large tree, bush and horse, large tree, he decided to let the two horses face the center tree. (Picture 47.) When he came to the design of the large tree, he drew his previous differentiated form (right-hand side of picture 45) on a piece of linoleum. His difficulties began when he started to cut it out; piece after piece broke off, and soon the design could not be used at all. "I have to make a simpler tree," he concluded, and in using a simpler configuration of form he came to the present design. When he drew the horse, he added a mane in a plain way but nevertheless followed a definite structural order. He drew a new shape for the horse's tail. (Picture 46.) Within the outline of the tail he drew the lines for the hair in a relation-

47. Michael's design to be used for a window curtain.

ship of direction to the outline. In the formation of the mane he applied the same principle. (Picture 47.)

The process of cutting out the figures in linoleum took him a long time, especially since it required careful work for the small details. He obviously had difficulty because his big, clumsy hands were not used to such delicate work. But he never asked for help, and proceeded slowly for two days. The printing was done in a simple manner. After the two blocks of linoleum were covered with oil colors blended with permanent mixture, the material was printed by hammering the blocks on it. Each block had to be fitted exactly to the neighboring one. In making the first two lines Michael needed help, but the rest he was able to do by himself. When he finished the last line, he expressed his satisfaction: "Gee, that's lots of fun. I should make one for my mother at home." And turning to the writer, he said: "When you go to New York tomorrow, will you go to my mother and ask her if she wants a curtain and find out how big she wants it? I want to make her one."[2]

After he had completed the window curtain, all his drawings were shown to him in the sequence of their production. He was obviously astonished, and could hardly believe that he had done them. This fact evidently must have impressed him. He, who was always sparing with words and had never spoken of his home, felt impelled to reveal a new aspect of his personality to his mother. Perhaps he wanted to make good at something, because he repeated his wish again, with the supplementary remark: "You see, when I write my mother it takes a couple of days till she gets my letter and it's hard for her to write. She's got lots to do." Self-respect, gained through productive work, created either a new or at least an increased relationship to his home, especially to his mother. He obviously felt a new worth within him which apparently he wanted to reveal to her.

A week later, Michael showed a drawing he had done over the week end, a rough sketch in which a horse was represented standing in front of a tree. When he was asked where he had got the idea, he said, "Out of my head." He wanted to enlarge the sketch to the size of his earlier large drawing and paint it with colors. He gave the horse a black color, and painted the branches brown and the leaves green. The mane of the horse underwent a small change: he gave the lines a wavy shape. But above all, whereas he had placed all his earlier horses against a light ground, this time he applied further the principle

---

[2] In accordance with the regulations of the institution, the author was not permitted to call on the mother.

of overlapping that had been attained in presenting the relationship between limbs and body, extending it even to the relationship of the whole horse to the bush in its background. Thus, further evidence is given of the spontaneous growth of Michael's inherent creative potentialities. (Picture 48.)

48. In the fifth month of his participation in the course, Michael applied overlapping to the entire design, placing a horse in front of a bush.

After he had completed this picture, he was asked for what purpose he would like to use it. He thought of making a large linoleum print. In order to stimulate his progress, reproductions of European folk art—hand-painted fabrics appropriate to his stage of development—were shown him. He immediately responded to these works and wanted to know how they had been made. Some of the fabrics, obviously meant for tablecloths, showed a figural frame around a central picture. After observing them for some time, he conceived the idea of using his previous design for a window curtain as a frame around his large picture of a horse. As the printing blocks were longer than

49. Michael's design for a printed fabric (36 by 36 inches).

the borders of the horse design, he found it necessary to enlarge the design at its lower end to accord with the size of the frame. But this made an empty space that bothered him. When he asked for advice, it was suggested that he fill it in with "some forms." He finally decided on a pattern of flowers and grass, much like that in the preceding picture.

The process of cutting this large design in linoleum took time. His interest in his work never decreased. When finally the day for printing came, he discovered that the four corners remained empty, and he decided to place a large tree in each corner to serve as a connecting link between the designs along the adjacent sides. The cutting out of these trees delayed the printing process for a whole week. The following week, Michael appeared nervous; he was worried about the appearance of the design on cloth. He insisted that he and John, another boy in the group, should together print the design. During this procedure, Michael displayed for the first time definite initiative. He told his friend how to handle the printing block exactly, how to hammer the different parts of the block, how to take it off the material, how to correct some places which were not clearly printed.

In comparison with the preceding picture of the same subject, this one (36 inches square) does not have the same vitality of expression. The difference was due to the process of linoleum cutting; the fine oscillations of the outlines in the former picture were now absent. However, this second picture has the charm of a real work of folk art. (Picture 49.) Michael was thoroughly conscious of his success, and again he expressed the wish to obtain permission to send his work to his mother. He seemed very much pleased with it at first. But the next day, when he had observed it again for a while, he said: "I don't like it as much as yesterday. There is something wrong with it." He was advised to study his work until he was able to find out the reason for his dissatisfaction. After about ten minutes he expressed definite disappointment: "I don't like it at all." Then suddenly he added: "It looks mixed up in back. The tree has too many branches." After he had examined the picture at length, he discovered that the clear form of the horse in the center was affected by the many branches, which appeared less organized. Agreeably surprised by Michael's discovery, which revealed that he was developing a definite visual judgment, the writer complimented him upon his observation. Asked what he wanted to do next, he replied: "I don't like to do it over again. I don't like to draw it again and cut it out again." But when he was asked if he wanted to try to make his horse in another material, such as a relief in clay to be cast later in artificial stone, he seemed encouraged.

A thick pane of glass the size of the center design, and some clay, were given him to work with. On one part of the glass the process of modeling was demonstrated. As soon as he understood this process, he set to work with enthusiasm. Using his eyes for visual observation and his hands for tactile observation, he constantly controlled his work by two different sense experiences and thus reached a greater perceptual comprehension of his object. Repeatedly saying, "This is fun," he obviously became more interested in his task. For hours he did not interrupt his work, not even to respond to his friends' conversation. Becoming more and more occupied by his project, his total organism—as a psychophysical whole—was made to function. This was clearly expressed when a definite movement of the modeling hands called forth a changing attitude of the rest of his body. His eyes, hands, constant visual and haptic judgment, his feeling and thinking, all became involved in his work. Continuing in this way, he roughly finished the figure of his horse by the end of the day. His parting remark pointed to his inner state: "I can hardly wait until next week."

For five weeks Michael was fully occupied with the perfecting of his relief in clay. In response to the author's frequent suggestions, he spent much time in thorough observation of his work in process. Often he changed the shape of the tree behind the horse. Each change caused a consequent change in other parts. In accomplishing his work he developed an independence of judgment that led to a definite inner security, most evident when other boys wanted to give him advice. Each time, he rejected all suggestions. He often became so angry at their interference that he threatened them. This young man, who experienced—perhaps for the first time—that he had definite abilities, and who felt that he could accomplish his own work as well as the others could accomplish theirs, attained strength to defend his product. Now he was not "lacking in confidence"; now he could "handle himself among more aggressive boys." There was nothing to be seen of his former "passive and timid" attitude.

Finally, after several weeks of work and again after long, thorough observation, he concluded: "I can't do any more. It's finished." The relief (18 by 22 inches in size) modeled in clay was cast in plaster of Paris, and from the negative plaster cast a positive cast in artificial stone was made. (Picture 50.)

In the course of the slow process of modeling, Michael achieved a completely new order within the form of the tree behind the horse. Through the character of the new material, clay, he was able to change the shape of his object until it had a simplicity that he could fully grasp. Whereas in the block print the tree with its leaves appeared confused to him (note the arbitrary overlapping of branches), he now carefully avoided any overlapping. In other words, he followed a definite principle of configuration already noted: in order to avoid confusion he regressed to an earlier stage of visual conception. Furthermore, in the earlier drawings as well as in the block print of the horse,

50. After six months of participation in the course, Michael accomplished this relief, "Horse in front of a bush," to be used as a sign for a stable.

Michael had represented overlappings only by lines. Now, by using clay, he could model overlapping; that is, he could realize it in terms of depth perception.

An evaluation of Michael's achievement as a work of art which not only attests to his mental accomplishment but also to his inner participation and to the change in him as a psychophysical whole—such an evaluation can be undertaken only by examining his work in relation to his own stage of development of visual conception. Any other consideration—such as comparison, in terms of naturalistic faithfulness to objects, with other works of art; or comparison of his work with work done on other artistic levels; or, as is common, evaluation by the standards of the observer's taste—cannot do justice to his production.

Observation of his work *on the basis of the pictorial data only* leads to the following judgment. Both figures—horse and tree—became satisfactorily visible. In spite of overlappings, all essential features are clearly shown. Any verbal explanation is superfluous. The figures can be distinctly recognized by observation only. The evolutionary process of creating the form of these figures has revealed that their structural organization is the result of Michael's visual conception and not of imitation of nature. In the construction of all forms, the stage of variability of direction is applied to all the main features; that is to say, parts are related to one another by similar angles. As we have already noted, the relationship between leaves and branches represents an earlier stage adopted in order to avoid confusion; and likewise with the lines of the hair in tail and mane. Furthermore, both figures are equally modeled. The most essential characteristics are realized. The figure of the horse, presented in its principal features, is placed against a background (tree) with more differentiated parts (leaves). This has the effect of a figure (horse) and a ground (tree) emphasizing each other in an interrelationship of form. But as the figure of the horse is the largest coherent unit in the picture, the not-so-coherent background serves to make the horse dominant in the subject matter. Form and content are thus indivisibly related. Finally, the picture reveals a uniformly applied relationship of variability of direction in all its parts. Even if the work is not a perfect unity of form, so far as the overlappings in the horse do not appear in the form of the bush, for an individual such as Michael, of designated low mentality, with extremely limited education and almost no opportunity for unfolding his inborn abilities, this work must be considered an extraordinary result.

Michael's work required, as has already been emphasized, a mental attitude that is characterized by intense unity in the function of all forces of visual conceiving: feeling, thought, will, and even physical concentration. This formative process, which involved his entire being, is organized mental activity of a high order. The organic unfolding of such energies may in turn lead to an increase of order and balance that are essential to the building of an integrated personality.

There was offered to Michael the possibility of gradually bringing inherent potentialities to bear. Step by step he achieved more difficult tasks which were in accordance with his natural capacities. His interest increased with the completion of new work. He gained faith in himself and simultaneously developed self-respect. Simple, clumsy drawings led to others with more differentiated configurations of form, which in turn mirrored his newly developed strength. Each consecutive effort opened possibilities for the realization of fresh ideas. He experienced an eagerness to work, as indicated by his remark, "I can hardly wait till next week." More and more courage and energy were released and transformed into a tangible reality. Gradually his inner security grew. He did not need advice from others. He became independent. His pictures became clearer and more vigorous in expression. His inner state is perhaps most clearly reflected in the upright attitude of his subject matter. (See the horse in picture 50.) The finished work and the creator merged into one indissoluble whole. The organized work, with its unified expression, throws light upon the present stage of his developing personality.

Six months passed between the first drawing and the final accomplishment of the relief in stone. At the end of this period Michael would still have five weeks in the institution before being paroled. It was left to him to decide how to utilize his time. He decided to make still another horse in clay, which he also wanted to see cast later in stone. But as the time for its accomplishment was very limited, a smaller size was chosen (11 by 20 inches). Michael started in a more or less playful way, working the clay into various shapes for his prospective figure of a horse. After a day's attempt he reached an approximate idea of his new work. Throughout the next two weeks his attitude was very different from what it had been previously. The exertion formerly displayed gave way to an easier working process. Although he showed the same initiative and perseverance, his second model did not require such stern effort. He conversed with other boys in the same group. Usually he entertained himself by whistling. When finally he seemed satisfied with his work, he displayed it to his friends—something he had not seemed willing to do before. They congratulated him and praised his work. But obviously he had not expected a spontaneous demonstration of that kind, and did not like it. He felt embarrassed and, withdrawing from the conversation, started to prepare plaster of Paris for the negative cast.

The next week, while the writer was absent from the institution, Michael obtained permission to cast the relief in artificial stone by himself. Then came his final week in the institution, the week of his parole. Throughout his last day in the course, he gave his full attention to his finished work (picture 51). He took it to a corner of the large workshop and observed it for some time.

51. After seven months of participation in the course, Michael achieved this, his last work, a relief (11 by 20 inches) modeled in clay and cast in artificial stone.

When he was informed that both reliefs in stone would be used for house-signs on the institution's grounds, a broad smile reflected his deep satisfaction.

A glance at Michael's last work shows at once how much it differs from all his previous efforts. The change in his behavior, from tense effort to relaxed, self-confident mastery of the artistic activity, is directly reflected in the strik-ing difference between the comparatively rigid forms of the previous works and the ease of attitude and freely modulating form in this one. Its simplicity gives the relief its profound expression. The stage of Michael's visual concep-tion—variability of direction—is harmoniously applied to the whole figure. Combined with this stage is the succeeding one, the stage of borderless transition from parts with figural meaning toward parts with ground meaning, through which the overlappings and the beginning of depth within the figure are realized. Furthermore, head and lifted leg are in a relationship of direction to each other by which the movement of the leg does not become an isolated part, but belongs to the whole figure. All previously applied stages of Michael's visual conception are merged into an indivisible organization of form. The subtle oscillation in the outline of the body—from hinder back to middle back, to neck, to head,—which recurs in the outline of the legs, gives a harmonious quality to the total picture.

The fluidity of expression in a completely configurated form reflects a normal man with a developed sensitivity and a constructive mind. There are no longer any signs of "deep feelings of inferiority." There is a secure will which forms and builds up. There is no longer a lack of confidence that leads to timidity and passivity. Michael's last work is documentary evidence of a consummation of an inner change—a change from an "apparently immature youth" to the maturity of a newly awakened creative personality.

Michael's development embraced a period of seven months. Here it must be noted that he had the opportunity of seeing horses on a few occasions, when the horse-drawn carts of the institution's farm were on the grounds; but the chances for observation were so brief that one can hardly consider them as exerting any essential influence upon his work. His progress must be attributed mainly to constant observation and visual judgment of each finished picture. With the repeated advice that he work out each picture as clearly as possible and carry it to completion, he gradually became able to determine which parts had to be changed in order to reach a perfection in which "all parts go together." Such a production must be recognized as an independent mental activity—the creation of relationships of form in the domain of visual conceiving. Each work conformed to what was then his stage of visual conception, until a new relationship of form became conceivable. Gradually the cognition of form in each new picture grew out of the cognition of form in the preceding one. Each stage of artistic development thoroughly set the condition for the next stage. This means that Michael's creative unfolding was the result of a natural growth of his inherent abilities. Only thus may be explained the achievement of so highly artistic a form in a comparatively limited time. "Where there is growth, there is motion, change, progress."[3] Its visible testi-

---

[3] John Dewey, *How We Think* (New York: Heath, 1910), pp. 194–195.

52. Relief of a rooster (9 by 12 inches) modeled in clay and cast in artificial stone, the work of an eighteen-year-old delinquent boy with an I.Q. of 96 and a grammar school education. He began in a very undeveloped way. His first drawing, of a farmhouse with chickens, corresponded approximately to the drawing of a normal seven-year-old child. This relief in artificial stone was done after three and a half months of participation in the course. The total visualization of the subject matter, its transformation into a simple, clear, unified form, gives to this work a quality that often appears in genuine productions of folk art.

mony, including all the social implications mentioned, is revealed in the comparison of Michael's last work with all his preceding ones.

On this and the following pages, pictures 52–59 show reliefs in stone, hand-printed fabrics, painted wall hangings, drawings, and a woodcarving, which exemplify achievements of other members of this experimental group of delinquents. It should be noted that, with two exceptions, all the boys started from the most primitive stage of visual conceiving.

53. Rooster (5 inches high) modeled in pottery clay and baked as a ceramic, then painted and baked again. This was done by the boy who made the relief of a rooster (picture 52). All parts—head, wings, feathers—are realized by the primary figure-ground relationship. They do not interfere with one another, and seen as a whole they become clearly visualized. In combination with the conformity in the tension of the entire outline, the unified structure of all parts gives a specific artistic value to this work. The same kind of structure can be found in many works of early epochs of art.

54. Hand-printed fabric; design representing "Dogs, bushes, flowers, and grass"; made by a twenty-two-year-old delinquent boy of low normal intelligence, after four months of participation in the course. This design was developed from simple drawings of dogs done with reference to the boy's own pet. As in all his previous works, spatial depth is realized in accordance with that early stage of visual conceiving in which objects are placed "above" and "below" each other without interference. This work demonstrates the fruitful utilization, for applied designs, of early stages of artistic formation.

55. Hand-painted fabric by the boy who produced the preceding design.

56. "Man Bowling," a relief (20 by 30 inches) cut in plaster of Paris and later cast in artificial stone, done by a delinquent boy eighteen years of age with an I.Q. of 90. Through the visualization of the whole figure, the coherent movement of all lines, and the uniform modeling of all parts, this work gains a quality found in much genuine folk art.

57. Wall hanging (6 by 3½ feet) painted in brown color by a delinquent youth of twenty-one with an I.Q. of 107, after four months of participation in the course. The pictorial construction of this design corresponds to that shown in picture 12. All figures and their details show distinctly the primary figure-ground relationship, and through the uniform application of variability of direction of lines the structure of this wall hanging attains a unity of form. It is by means of this unity of form that the maker of this work grasps and expresses his idea artistically.

58. "Sugar-plantation Worker Sharpening His Knife"; a woodcarving (5 by 1¾ feet) done by a delinquent Puerto Rican twenty years of age with an I.Q. of 80 and a sixth-grade elementary school education. This young man, who had worked as a seaman for four years, had a special interest in handicrafts and had executed some simple woodcarving. He also had a well-developed power of visual conceiving; his first drawing showed already advanced stages. The pictorial realization of this comparatively complicated work was prepared by means of many drawings, until his idea of the subject matter became totally visible in an orderly fashion. This woodcarving was done after he had participated in the course five months.

59. "A Desolate Landscape," pencil drawing (10 by 13 inches) done by a twenty-year-old delinquent youth with an I.Q. of 106. He was a sensitive, ambitious young man, had little contact with other inmates of the institution, and preferred to be alone. His repeated saying, "I hate cities, I like desolation," may explain his selection of this theme, drawn after he had participated for five months in the course.

Because he had copied pictures, his ability in visual conceiving was little developed. By constant application of visual judgment he clarified his drawings more and more until he gradually found his own manner of artistic expression. The main structures of this drawing reveal variability of direction of lines, which is governed, in turn, by a unified relationship of direction. It is by this means that the picture becomes visually consistent. The same principle of order is attained in the formation of the rocks of the cliffs. Their outlined shapes reflect a particular feeling for their characteristics whereby the difference in the substance of the rock formations and earth formations is pictorially realized.

In all parts of the picture the idea of spatial depth is especially stressed by shaded overlapping, which shows unified application of the borderless transition from parts with figural meaning to parts with ground meaning. This complicated subject matter becomes visually graspable through a highly organized structural unity which, in turn, conveys successfully the artistic feeling of its originator.

Chapter Five

THE EXPERIMENT
WITH REFUGEES

THE EXPERIMENT with refugees was started in the summer of 1939 and was continued for three years. The group included five refugees, of various occupations: a former lawyer, forty-three years of age, who became an adviser to an export firm in this country; a musician and conductor thirty-six years old; a housewife of thirty-five; a physiotherapist of thirty; and a twelve-year-old girl. The lawyer and the musician had to discontinue after one year, owing to occupational pressures, and the housewife had to discontinue after two years in order to accept an income-producing position. The group met one night weekly for two hours.

The development of Miss R. B., the physiotherapist, is chosen to demonstrate this experiment.

Miss B was thirty years of age when she entered the experimental course. She had come to the United States in the fall of 1933. She was born in Berlin, where she attended a municipal high school for girls until her sixteenth year. Subsequently she took a course in physical education and became a teacher in that field. According to her own written statement concerning her previous experience in art, she participated in the art classes in her school but was "not particularly inspired by the instruction." She continues: "For a few years I was a regular Sunday visitor to the different art museums in Berlin. I think my visits did not mean much to me; perhaps for reasons of social requirements cultured people were expected to know something about art. Many years after I had left school I was primarily interested in the modern dance and physical education. My present profession as physiotherapist developed from these interests. Years ago, a friend of mine who was not able to draw attended some art classes and found that she possessed artistic ability. That was an inspiration to me. Since that time there was always the question in my mind why I was not also able to do so. From the time I have been in the United

States, I have been working as a physiotherapist in a New York hospital. The work was so hard that after treating patients all day I could not continue dancing as a hobby. But I always felt that I had to do some kind of creative work." Miss B was introduced to the group by a friend who had already participated for a few weeks.

At the first lesson she examined the works of the others. She showed great interest, especially as she seemed able to appreciate the pictorial results of the others who were at that time at an undeveloped artistic stage. When the group broke up for the evening, Miss B remarked that she would like to do something of her own over the week end and bring it in at the following lesson.

The next week, Miss B brought with her a small head modeled in clay, 5 inches in height (picture 60). "I had some clay left over," she said, "which I used in a pottery class at the Harlem Art Center of the W. P.A. I attended a class for a few weeks. As I was always interested in modeling, it came naturally to my mind to attempt to model. I tried to make first a head because it would be easier than a whole figure." While she was displaying the work, she was requested to express her opinion about it. She said: "The face is too flat. The mouth looks like it was smiling—it looks funny. I think I will try to make another one and change the shape of the face." The other participants of the group responded encouragingly to her first work and urged her to continue. "For this reason," she remarked, "I always looked forward to meeting this group."

Miss B's first work reflects an early stage of visual conceiving, such as is found in similar works of primitive art. The flat plane of the front of the head is a secure basis for the formation of eyes, nose, and mouth. Eyes and nose are in a clear relationship of the greatest contrast of direction to each other, while the shape of the mouth is determined by a definite relationship of direction to the outline of the lower part of the head. Through this latter relationship the mouth obtains an expression which can easily be interpreted as smiling, but which was not Miss B's intention. As she was obviously not able to conceive the mouth line in a relationship of direction to three objects—nose and two eyes,—she solved this problem in a simpler way by seeing it in relationship to only one object, the contour of the lower part of the head. In other words, she regressed to an early stage of visual conception, that of lines in relationship of direction to each other.[1] (See the formation of tail and mane

_____

[1] This structure of form appears frequently in all epochs of archaic and primitive art.

60. Miss B's first modeled head.

in picture 48.) "Smiling" as an expression would have affected the structural relationship of all the features of the face, a change which in turn would have required a more complicated visual conception. The horizontal-vertical coherence between eyes and nose, and the relationship of direction between the mouth and lower part of the head, form the "face." The face, therefore, is the pictorial result of conceiving visually the different parts in definite relationships of form to one another.

It is easy to understand why Miss B did not feel satisfied with her first modeled work. The form of this head is so far removed from her conceptual knowledge of the object that it inevitably caused a conflict in her mind. Nevertheless, this primitive work reveals a genuine, even though very modest, beginning of artistic configuration. This simple order of form became a natural basis from which Miss B could develop further her abilities. Such an independent development could only take place by her critical observation of her finished work, out of which a new idea for a new work could emerge.

The execution of her second head, which is of the same size as the first, took considerably longer. She worked more slowly, and as she was advised to observe her object frequently, she stopped more often in order to judge her work. When the work was finished, it was cast in artificial stone. (Picture 61.)

In this new head the flat face has disappeared: the head is modeled in the round. The face has obtained a more unified form because eyes, nose, and mouth are held together by the greatest contrast of direction, whereby the whole attains a more rigid as well as tranquil expression. It must be noted that this expression is the result of her particular stage of visual conception and not of imitation of nature. The rigidity in the expression is further emphasized by the prominence of the upper and lower eyelids as well as of the lips. The stressing of such parts is prompted only by an inner urgency to obtain the best visual comprehension possible. At this comparatively undeveloped stage of visual conception the only other means for reaching a clear visual understanding are stresses on the most essential features of the object. Eyes, nose, and mouth exist separately and are distinctly set off from their surrounding ground. All these characteristics are typical of primitive art forms.

Miss B was requested to observe thoroughly her second work and to make suggestions for a new one. She soon expressed the intention of making "a head of a girl—bigger—so that I can model the hair also." In the same lesson she finished a rough outline of her new work, which was 10 inches in height.

61. Miss B's second modeled head.

She spent several weeks on it because of the limited time she could give to the execution of this head and because of her slow and careful procedure.

Finally, her accomplished product (picture 62) was placed on a bookshelf. She criticized it as follows: "As a whole the head looks quite stylized—like a mask. The lines of the hair are too even. The eyes seems to be too big. The mouth has too sharp an outline. This reminds me of a head of an early Greek sculpture."

It is interesting to note that during the several weeks when Miss B concentrated on shaping the details of her third work she was not aware of her "quite stylized" head that looked "like a mask." She emphasized as before the most essential characteristics of her object. She again organized the relationship of eyes and nose in accordance with the horizontal-vertical principle. In forming the mouth she tended to revert to the coherence of direction seen in her first head. This relationship of direction is also applied to the formation of the hair; that is, the strands are organized as a pattern of parallel units. In sum, a definite order of form has resulted. All that she did was governed by her inner need of grasping visually the variety of shapes by structural organization. This creative operation was again determined by her stage of visual conception, previously mentioned. The process took full possession of her and became so strong that her criticisms about the "stylized head," the evenness of hair, the large size of the eyes, and so on, could not enter her consciousness while she was engrossed in her work. Her creative activity manifested itself as so dynamic a mental action that once she was on the way to artistic production she had to follow through. Interference by any other thought could not take place. The beginning of conceiving relationships of form demanded consistent execution of that activity.

After judging her finished work, she soon found it necessary to change it entirely. As a result of her critical attitude she received stimulation for a new pictorial idea, and thus she grew through her work. The intended change of form of her work was predetermined by a change within herself, best expressed in her own words: "Whenever I come to the group and see my works, I do not like them any more. I find when I see them again that I have to change a lot."

Miss B's criticism of her modeling ended, as we have noted, in the remark: "This reminds me of a head of an early Greek sculpture." For the first time she seemed to see a comparison of her stage of visual conception with that of a

62. Miss B's third modeled head.

63. Early Greek head, from about the first quarter of the sixth century B.C.

similar one of an early epoch of art. As this offered the possibility of furthering such a comparison, she was requested to study the illustrations of the book *L'Art en Grèce*[2] and to write down her impressions. After observing the pictures in this book, she formulated the results of her discoveries as follows: "I found a few heads which look very similar to the one I made. [See picture 63.] The similarity lies in the shape of the hair, the big pronounced eyes, and the shape of the mouth. Both heads, the one I made as well as the one I noticed in particular, have, peculiarly, smiling mouths. I did not intend to make such a smiling mouth. In fact, it was a great surprise when I finished the head. I assume that the smiling in the illustrated head was not intended, either. Through the connection I found between my work and early Greek sculptures a great interest was aroused in me for the art of that time."

This statement indicates that appreciation of works of art having structural forms that are closely related to those created by oneself may lead to an understanding of essential artistic values. Finding works of historic art that resembled her own achievements may have given Miss B some insight into the significance of her own production. As her inherent abilities progressed, this creative approach was continued.

"I want to make a head that looks more vital," said Miss B, before starting her fourth work. The lump of clay she chose for the rough outline was bigger than the previous one. She was advised to interrupt, to observe, and to judge her work frequently, while modeling this larger head. Proceeding thus, she gave almost three months to the accomplishment of the new head.

The finished work, revealing the same stage of visual conception as the former one, is different in its expression. In spite of its simplicity, Miss B's intention to make this work "more vital" is clearly realized. (Picture 64.) This vitality must be attributed to the fact that eyes, nose, and mouth are not emphasized as independent single objects. Through a certain smoothness in their shapes they merge into the head. They give up their single existences and become inseparable from the whole head. In other words, the distinct borders of these facial features, strongly set off from their surrounding ground (as seen in the earlier heads), give way to the beginning of the borderless transition from figural meaning to ground meaning. Furthermore, a smoothness of the mass of the hair, a greater differentiation of the forehead, whereby the left and the right sides appear, and finally a division of the lips, contribute

---

[2] Christian Zervos, *L'Art en Grèce* (2d ed.; Paris: Cahiers d'Art, 1936).

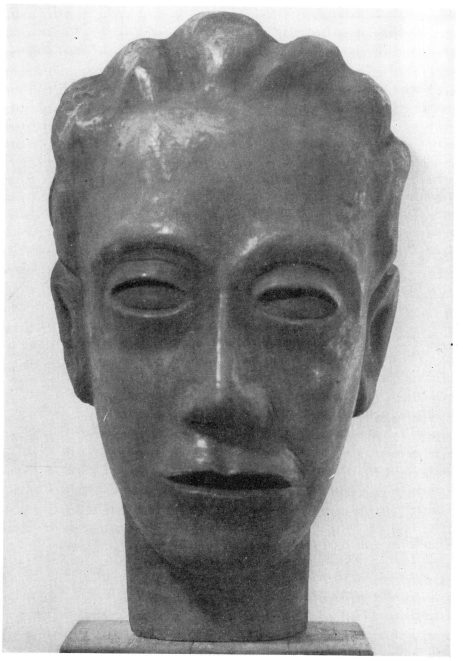

64. Miss B's fourth modeled head.

essentially to the vitalization of the whole head. After long observation, Miss B made the following conclusive statement: "This looks much more as I want it. It really gives me much pleasure to see it. It pays to work hard even if it is sometimes difficult."

Her remarks demonstrate the effect which this creative work had upon her. In her writing about her lessons as well as her art work at home she affirms: "Very often, after a hard day's work, it became an effort for me to go to the art group. I was then so tired that I felt I would not be able to do anything. But as I was anxious to proceed with my work I forced myself to go. Usually it was a surprise to me to experience that, after a few minutes of concentration on my work, my tenseness and tiredness gradually disappeared. My mental and physical state changed entirely. In fact, I felt I could do many hours of work again. I usually modeled a long time and only stopped because of the late hours, but not because I was tired. Sometimes, even after I had left the group at night, my wish to go on became so great that I continued to work at home until very late."

There is, of course, nothing new in the stimulating effect of recreational activity. Nevertheless, it seems worth while to consider the possibility that the effect of this specific kind of occupation may go far beyond that attained by common leisure-time activities. The making of such a modeled head is of a productive, creative character. The mental concentration required by the task produces its well-known tonic effect. It is important to realize that this activity is constantly stimulated by the task itself, which calls for the attainment of perfection. "The nearer we are to perfection, the stronger is the need to perform."[3] This incentive will be particularly strong because the work is not imposed upon the individual, but is conceived or begotten by him. It springs from essential characteristics and needs of the personality and spontaneously expresses them.

Nine months had passed since Miss B entered the course. From simple beginnings she progressed to her present stage. This progress was based upon constant self-criticism. One result always determined the achievement of the following one. Since she did not find it necessary to change anything in her latest work, it seemed to be in closest conformity with her ability in creative configuration. One day the four heads she had made were displayed in the sequence of their development. They must have given her great satisfaction

---

[3] Kurt Goldstein, *Human Nature* (Harvard University Press, 1940), p. 147.

and incentive for further activity, because she expressed herself as follows: "After seeing a great progress from the first very simple head to the present one I have courage enough to start a whole figure. I am aware it can only be one with very plain forms. I would like to make a standing woman in a simple dress."

Miss B's intention of making a whole figure of a standing woman, "one with very plain forms," indicates that she knew the difficulty of creating a unified work. Therefore, she does not pretend to realize a complicated subject matter the artistic solution of which might be beyond her abilities. She planned to achieve her utmost within the frame of her artistic potentialities. Her new statue (picture 65) is 20 inches in height. Simple as it is, all its parts display a definitiveness and clearness that have their origin in her determination to accomplish the most convincing visual form. In spite of archaic rigidity, a smoothness, already expressed in the head previously modeled, glides over the whole work. Life seems to have entered this figure—a lifelike quality which is evident in all early works of art that have just evolved out of the sternness of the primitive form. This vitality is the result of a slight but harmonious application of the stage of variability of direction, best expressed by the attitude of the arms and also reflected in the light oscillation of all contours. The movement of the arms does not endanger the uniformity of the whole work. The arms are attached to the body in such a way that they join the wholeness of the figure. Let us say, the sculptural quality of the total form is maintained. Further attention must be given to the particular way in which the lower right arm crosses over the dress just as the right hand overlaps the left arm. The lower right arm is distinctly set off from its ground, the dress. The right hand overlaps the left arm and divides it in two equal parts so that the left arm not only serves as the clearest ground meaning to the right hand, but itself remains convincingly recognizable. In the sculpturing of both arms a figure-ground relationship has been created that contributes decisively to the plain visual comprehension of the whole figure.

It is obvious that so complicated a task could not have been achieved in a short time. The execution of this work required a few months, but Miss B gave at most no more than a few evening hours a week to it. During this period she was again repeatedly requested to watch the process of modeling very carefully and to write down all her essential experiences. The following is a summary of her observations.

65. Miss B's fifth work. At left, front view; at right, side view.

"Modeling a figure, I found out that every little touch brought an absolute change. After the form kept changing over and over I realized that I had to keep my eyes constantly on the whole figure and not just on the part I was working on. From time to time I had to step back and look at it from a distance; only then did I get the impression of the figure as one piece and not as consisting of separate parts. It was a new experience for me that this kind of work demanded so much concentration. Not only the eyes and the hands coördinated; sometimes I felt that my whole body was doing the work This must be the reason that I always felt like a different person when I was modeling."

The fact that a layman who does not intend to enter the artistic profession obtains an understanding of essential aspects of the artistic procedure through his own spontaneous experience should not be underestimated. This fact becomes even more significant if one keeps in mind how little the educated person knows about the essence of artistic creation. Even when some such knowledge is acquired by psychological studies or philosophical contemplation, a noteworthy gap still exists between knowledge gained by conceptual considerations and that attained by even partial insight resulting from one's own concrete experience. It is no secret that many learned scholars and critics of aesthetics and art often become embarrassed when, confronted with a work of art, they face the task of explaining their knowledge about artistic qualities. They may well be able to explain external rules of composition, or essential historical characteristics, or to interpret symbolic meanings; but the definite structural organization, the artistic form, or, as Miss B expressed it in her simple terms, "the figure as one piece and not as consisting of separate parts," is very seldom a familiar subject to such art connoisseurs. All philosophical, historical, or psychological interpretations of a work of art are inadequate where the innermost core of art is concerned. Miss B's case indicates that there is no better way to grasp essential values of a work of art and inner acquaintance with the artistic process than through an intelligent observation of one's own artistic procedure. As Goethe stated it: "One can only grasp what one can produce oneself."[4]

For some weeks Miss B was absent from the course. When she returned she submitted the following report on visits she had made to museums.

"I have been at the Metropolitan Museum of Art a few times just to look at some sculptures, since through my own art experience I am most interested

---

[4] In a letter to the composer Karl Friedrich Zelter, Director of the Berlin Singing Academy, March 28, 1803.

66. Miss B's sixth work.

in them. I was very happy to find among the early Greek sculptures some statuettes which resembled very much the statue of a woman I had made myself. In these statuettes I found a great simplicity, a certain stiffness, and simple lines that make each figure into an harmonious piece. Similar sculptures with the same characteristics are displayed in the rooms of Egyptian art. My visits to the museum gave me an idea for a new sculpture."

The statement just quoted shows clearly that Miss B's visits to an art museum now had personal significance for her. They were induced by a definite interest in art and were no longer undertaken, as years ago, "for reasons of social requirements." The museum became a source for the spontaneous enrichment of her knowledge of the history of art. As she found works of art related to her own achievement, the faith in her productive worth increased and became a source of happiness. The features of ancient works of art spoke her own artistic language. A consciousness of a mental kinship with those who had come to similar artistic results may have dawned in her. In this spirit she conceived the idea for a new work. The museum lost its meaning as a place for a mere accumulation of artistic objects. Its treasures became decisive incentives to the unfolding of creative energies.

In comparison with her previous statue, this one (picture 66), 9 inches in height, is more differentiated, but nevertheless it has a perfect unity of form. The scarf, supplying ground meaning for the head, sets off the head distinctly. The same scarf in its downward extension carries the function of figural meaning to the chest, where it covers shoulders and arms. There the scarf brings out the chest, and vice versa. This relationship is so precisely balanced that both parts are convincingly visible. Through a large fold which divides equally the lower part of the modeling a plain, clear structure of the skirt is attained. Moreover, the outline of the whole figure as well as of its parts indicates in its light oscillation a sensitive application of the stage of variability of direction. All these factors taken together give this figure a uniform visual order, a genuine artistic quality.

The great simplicity and clearness of form in Miss B's sculpture are closely connected with like qualities in many works of contemporary art. A possibility of becoming acquainted with modern sculptures thus presented itself to her. For this purpose a series of photographs representing works of various sculptors was shown her. She appreciated many of them, but, as her statement reveals, she was most of all impressed by the art of Ernest Barlach.

67. Two views of Miss B's seventh work.

"I like the plainness of Barlach's figures very much. Their few folds do not disturb these figures, but underline their whole movement. I am under the impression that I would possibly work in a similar way. There is something I admire most in Barlach's works—though he usually dresses his figures entirely, I can still see the movement of the form of the body. Though I have seen many famous sculptures in different museums—I think for instance of those of Rodin and casts of Michelangelo's work in the Metropolitan Museum of Art,—I must confess that I don't understand them because their great multiplicity of shapes is utterly confusing to me. However, seeing the works of Barlach, I can say that I really enjoy them because the plainness in each piece enables me to understand them perfectly."

This brief statement may again indicate how an approach to works of art based on an individual's creative experience leads to understanding and enjoyment of artistic products which are related to his own accomplishments. Such an understanding opens a way to genuine appreciation of specific artistic stages of early and modern epochs.

Once Miss B had learned, from experience, how to achieve a relatively complicated artistic task, she found more courage and determination. Her last preceding work now stimulated her to make a new though similar statue. Her statement, "I want to make another figure of a woman in a similar dress but larger and with more movement," pointed to her new idea.

The creation of this new figure, 24 inches in height (picture 67), required several months of work and demanded a vigorous functioning of all her energies. Because of her intention to express greater movement throughout the entire sculpture, she was forced to a constant, tense observation. Each particular accomplishment had to be judged in its relation to the expression of the whole figure. The solution of this problem often seemed so difficult that Miss B was several times inclined to give up. The problem was further complicated by the fact that she could not give her full time to its execution, for with the continual interruption of a week between each two work periods she always needed a long time to regain intimacy with the growing artistic structure. But at last there came an evening when, after protracted critical observation and comparison with her previous work, she found full satisfaction and declared her work finished. The clay model was cast in artificial stone.

If one judges the value of works of art according to their artistic form, a distinction between the greater and the less developed ones will always be difficult, if not often impossible. A work of early Egyptian sculpture may have in its simple structure a quality of form equal to that of a highly differentiated Gothic figure of Christ. The difference consists in the two varying stages of artistic configuration, but not in quality. From this point of view, the concept "artistic development" does not seem fitting. This attitude cannot, of course, be taken if one considers the production of a single individual as the unfolding of his artistic potentialities. His particular achievement, especially if it reflects an early artistic stage, may be a perfect work of art, and yet his artistic potentiality may well be able to master more complex tasks which in turn would require greater creative power. It is this point of view which may justify the characterization of Miss B's new figure of a woman as a more developed work of art than the preceding one. The whole figure reveals a greater but a uniform application of the stage of variability of direction. In effect, all lines gain a certain vitality of expression: a definite, tense oscillation governs the entire work. All contours of the dress are related to one another through a unity of direction which gives the whole figure a visual clearness and firmness in construction and points to the fact that it is a product, not of uncontrolled feelings, but of highly disciplined sensitivity.

Miss B became more and more aware of her inborn artistic potentialities, of which she had previously been ignorant. Together with this consciousness, an increasing self-evaluation of her artistic production was evident. Each time she entered the studio and before she started to work, she spent some time enjoying her productions. She did the same before she left for home. Her finished results seemed to become the visible documentations of her creative nature; she thus felt a certain happiness in the nearness of her works. It was natural, therefore, that she wanted to have her productions in her home.

The display of her sculptures in her room gave it a strong personal note. In order to round out this impression more completely, and because she was stimulated by other participants in the course who made hand-printed fabrics, Miss B decided to design a wall hanging. She drew different trees, bushes, flowers, and grass, all of which represented the stage of variability of direction of lines. As these designs were not too complicated, they could easily be cut in linoleum blocks which in turn would serve as printing blocks. After the completion of two different trees and flowers, and one design for the bushes, a total theme had to be chosen. The most familiar idea, naturally, was "A garden with trees, bushes, and flowers." When the entire design was laid out in a sketch on a large sheet of paper, Miss B bordered it above and below with a fence. Nevertheless, she was not satisfied; but neither was she able to find the reason for her dissatisfaction. A week later she brought in a drawing, "Sweethearts sitting on a bench." This more vital theme was added and placed in the center of the whole design.

68. Hand-printed fabric (48 by 36 inches) done by Miss B.

The park bench with two lovers represents a new element of form. (Picture 68.) Its structure is built upon a different application of the variability of direction of lines (demonstrated in picture 13). The spatial appearance of the bench is attained by joining the lines of the left and the right borders of the surface to the vertical legs of the bench by means of slanting lines. The angle of the joint is applied in turn to all four corners, and thus the lower starting point of the back legs appears to be "higher," or farther back. The sitting position of the two lovers is also determined by the slanting lines of the borders of the surface; that is to say, the upper legs of the man and the outline of the skirt of the girl are in a parallel relationship of direction to the left and right slanting lines. This new structure is (as already demonstrated in our statement of theory) an advanced kind of spatial representation in comparison with the primary one, which is marked by organizing objects "above and below" and "side by side."

The printed fabric must have contributed to an even greater awareness of a self-created environment. Miss B's happiness also increased when friends and relatives who visited her home appreciated her work. But one day an event occurred that was of particular importance to her. As she reports it:

"One day when I was not feeling well and had to call in a doctor, I had the greatest surprise. When he entered my room, which is a furnished room in a rooming house, the first thing he asked me was if I had a boy friend who is an artist. Before I could tell him that I had made all the heads and figures and the wall hanging myself, he told me he liked them very much. I never thought of myself as an artist, but when the doctor left my home and once more assured me how much he enjoyed these different pieces, it gave me much pleasure. The fact that a stranger recognized and praised the quality of my works had a personal meaning to me. It made me feel of particular worth. I had received similar praise before by some of my friends, which might have been friendly or flattering, but that a complete stranger took the same attitude made me very proud of myself."

The social significance of being recognized as a creative individual cannot be overestimated. Such recognition reflects back upon the creator's self-esteem and makes him realize that he has something unique to give. To that which characterized him before, a new and vital trait has been added. He has acquired new status. He feels more accepted. This furthers self-confidence and at the same time stimulates him to do more, for he knows he has much more within him to bring forth as his own, which in turn will bring him yet more recognition.

Following the completion of her wall hanging, Miss B again returned to her modeling. After studying her two standing figures, she felt impelled to concentrate once more on a single head, "much larger than the others, in life size," and with particular emphasis on "expression of eyes, nose, mouth," and so on. She intended to work on it as long as should be necessary to reach full satisfaction. The work required four months (one evening a week) for its completion.

The impressive character of this work (picture 69) is mainly called forth by a distinct application of the figure-ground relationship to all its parts. The

69. Miss B's eighth work.

shape of the hair surrounds the face in such a way that both are very clearly set off from each other; the simple modeled planes of the face form a strong contrast to the ornament of the hair. Within the ground meaning of the face, all essential parts—eyes, nose, mouth—attain figural meaning, but they do not exist singly; their border with figural meaning passes gradually over into the ground meaning of the face. The same relationship is evident between forehead and cheeks, and between cheeks and lower part of the face. This means that while the entire sculpture is clearly accentuated by its principal parts, which carry figural meaning, they all belong inextricably together because of a harmonious application of the stage of borderless transition from parts with figural meaning to parts with ground meaning. Furthermore, the way in which the principle of form just described is applied points to a consistent application of the specific language of form found in the two previous works. In other words, the particular expression of movement achieved in the figures of the standing women appears also in the formation of this head. This is demonstrated by the oscillating outlines of the entire figure, beginning with the wavy shape of the hair and the slight curves of the forehead, which pass over into the tense bending of the contour of the nose and are continued in the shape of the upper lip and finally end in the sweeping curve of the chin. The same feeling of form is apparent not only in the outlines that go from upper to lower parts, but also in those that go from one side to the other. This particular expression is not possible unless it includes in well-balanced function the stage of variability of direction of lines which operate in a constant relationship of direction. In sum, the equal application of all the principles of form described in this chapter make this head a configurated whole in which each part receives its structural meaning only in its relation to this whole. Thus the subject matter, "head," does not exist without configurated form; moreover, it attains its real meaning through the artistic form.

At the time this report is written, the modeled "head" is Miss B's latest ac-complishment, but her repeated assurance, "I will never stop my artistic work," may indicate that her activity has become an indispensable factor in her life: because, as she stated in her own written account, "it gave me something I needed badly after so many working hours; and further, it opened to me a complete new world which, though I knew about it, I never believed that I would ever have entrance to it."

The unfolding of Miss B's artistic activity may demonstrate what creative potentialities are planted in a human being. It can be said without exaggeration that there is hardly a normal person who could not start in the way she did. What may seem more surprising is the fact that she was able to reach these particular artistic heights through the achievement of only eight modeled works. This may find its explanation in the fact that her first work revealed already a very simple but unadulterated artistic construction of form which became the basis for all further steps of her creative unfolding. Her creative powers were never misdirected by external influences which were not suited to her stages of artistic development. Each performance was perfected according to her current, temporary abilities; that is to say, it was the result of her temporary stage of visual cognition. Each finished work supplied the elements for the construction of the following one, and as her production was always in innermost connection with her genuine experience, she and her work grew organically. She was constantly her own best witness of this growth. Under such conditions she received deep satisfaction and enjoyment, and faith and courage for new and higher creative ventures.

70. Design for lace (14 by 13 inches) done by Mrs. N.M., a dressmaker thirty-seven years of age, after nine months of participation in the course. Stimulated by seeing pigeons daily, Mrs. M did several drawings and watercolors, a painting on glass, and a modeled relief representing birds. From the beginning, she showed special interest in the various patterns of feathers, which she developed into harmonious designs. Her artistic ability remained predominantly at the stage of two-dimensional conception of space. Within this restriction she developed a great variety of different designs.

71. "Deer with trees and bushes," another applied design (14 by 13 inches) done by
Mrs. M, after one year of participation in the course.

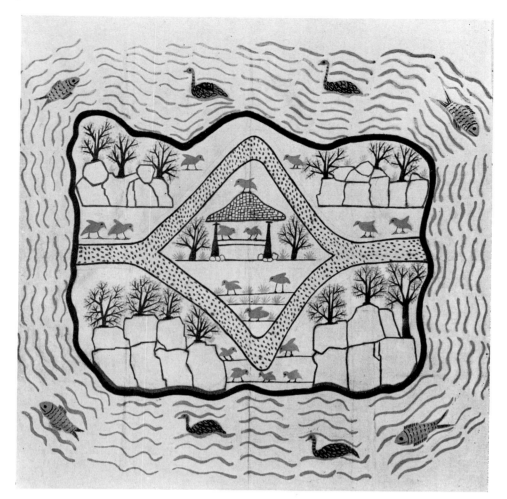

72. "Bird Island in Central Park," a painted wall hanging (38 by 38 inches) done by Mr. B, a man forty-three years of age, formerly a lawyer, who became an adviser to an export business in this country. This work was done after he had participated for seven months in the course. Mr. B, who showed great interest in maps, began to draw a map of Manhattan; but as he encountered difficulties, he limited the subject matter more and more until he arrived at this representation. The island, as an outlined and directed intentional figure, is surrounded by waves, fish, and swimming birds, which together carry the meaning of water. A path crosses the island. All the figures, even the groups of rocks, are placed on horizontal base lines. The surface of the rocks takes over the function of such base lines in relation to the trees placed on top of them. All the figures are in a unity of direction to one another.

73. "Self-portrait in Central Park," a watercolor (40 by 30 inches) done by Miss N.M., fourteen years of age, after she had participated for two years in the course. Throughout the picture all objects are realized in their total shapes. There is a unified application of the principle of variability of direction of lines in the structure of all the main parts as well as of their details, which all together are governed by a unified relationship of direction. Overlapping of hills, arms, and body indicate the beginning of a more complicated idea of spatial depth.

74. "Two Friends Shaking Hands," a pencil drawing (22 by 28 inches), another work by Miss N.M., done when she was fifteen. The stiffness in the attitude of the body seen in the preceding picture has given way to a certain vitality in these two human figures. This fact can only be attributed to a more extended application of the principle of variability of direction of lines to both figures. In addition, borderless transition from parts with figural meaning to parts with ground meaning, emphasized by shade and light, reveals Miss M's new idea of spatial depth in the formation of hair, eyes, and nostrils, and the folds of the dresses, as well as in the relationship of the human figures to the trees.

75. "Self-portrait," a pencil drawing (11 by 8½ inches) done by Miss N.M. at the age of sixteen. The sensitive oscillations of all outlines of this drawing indicate an increase in the application of variability of direction of lines. Single parts, such as mouth, nose, eyes, and hair, attain greater independent expression. The structure of the hair, the relationship between forehead and hair, between the eye and its surroundings, between nostrils and cheek, upper and lower lip, chin and neck, and finally between one and another fold of the dress, reveal an intelligent organization of light and shade for the sake of a greater spatial appearance. Miss M reaches an artistic stage of development which has many analogous examples in the art of the early Italian Renaissance, as well as in Indian portraits of the sixteenth century.

76. "Orchestra," a pencil drawing (10 by 12 inches), the first work of Mr. H.W., a musician and conductor thirty-six years of age. The development of Mr. W's pictorial activity is shown because he started differently from the other participants in this group. Like many adult beginners, he began with an extended subject matter which he could only memorize in the simplest way. He showed the arrangement of the various musicians in the orchestra, but he only indicated the figures by simple dots and lines—except those in the top row, for which he indicated their essential movements.

77. "Cello Player," Mr. H.W.'s second drawing. After observing his first drawing for a short time, Mr. W became aware of his unsatisfactory result and decided to draw a single cello player. However, he again rendered a special pose of his subject which in its complication and confused lines did not give him visual satisfaction.

78. "Cello Player," Mr. H.W.'s third drawing. When the pencil drawing of this figure was completed, it was suggested to Mr. W that he fill in its outlines with black ink for the purpose of attaining a better visual judgment. In spite of a clearer rendering of his subject, he did not like the "arrangement of arms, their connection to the cello, and the large head of the cello player." He proceeded with a number of new drawings by which he intended to reach a more satisfactory result.

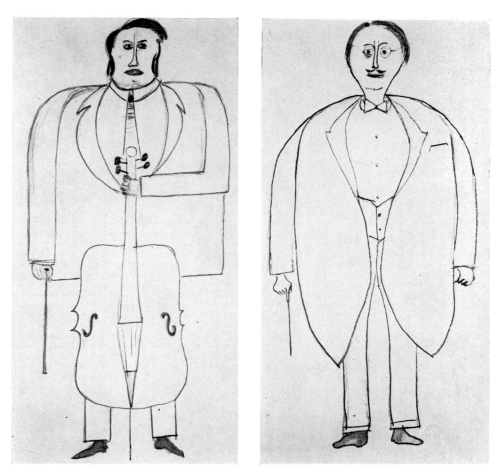

79. "Cello Player."   80. "Conductor."

This "Cello Player" is the first drawing by Mr. W which satisfied him. In comparison with his earlier pictures, it gives a more immediate presentation of the total figure of a cello player. A simple solution of spatial depth is expressed by the overlapping of the left arm and chest, as well as the upper part of the cello and the legs and lower part of the jacket. However, the main structure of this figure reveals a visual organization which is in accordance with the greatest contrast of direction of lines. Even in the formation of the face this principle of form is evident; the horizontally directed eyes are attached directly to the vertical lines of the nose.

The orderly arrangement of the parts in the earlier drawings as piecemeal imitative renderings of natural impressions led to distorted, unclear figures. In effect, these drawings were not visually comprehensible to Mr. W and therefore were unsatisfactory. The structure of this drawing, on the contrary, is the result of a simple though clear visual conception of the total object and consequently gave Mr. W visual satisfaction.

The drawing (picture 80) entitled "Conductor," one of many similar drawings, exemplifies Mr. W's visual comprehension of his idea. The subject is represented in its total shape, and through a structural order of all its parts it is elevated into a primitive artistic form.

81. "Quintet of Musicians" (20 by 18 inches). Six colored tiles made by Mr. W after six months of participation in the course. In order to obtain a more tangible perceptual result of his pictorial ideas, Mr. W acted upon a suggestion that he should model some of his figures into flat reliefs of clay, later to be cast in plaster of Paris. He selected five musicians and a conductor. He finally expressed a wish to color his figures in order to see his idea better. The simple, unadulterated configuration of the entire work gives it a quality found in many productions of genuine folk art.

82. "Violin Player."   83. "A Conductor."

The "Violin Player" is a relief (15 by 12 inches) modeled in clay, cast in plaster of Paris, and colored. After critical observation of the previously accomplished relief of the "Quintet," Mr. W liked best the form of the woman violin player. He decided to concentrate on this subject and develop it further. Through his efforts he reached a rigid but distinct formation of this figure. In spite of the more differentiated shape of the dress, the main structure of this relief is based upon the horizontal-vertical relationship of form. In the configuration of the hair a definite relationship of direction to the outline of the head is evident. The same principle of form exists in the relationship of the curved outline of the chin and the curved shape of the lower lip.

Stiff and primitive as this work may look, it is the creative result of a transformation of the manifold shapes of this object in nature into a visually organized whole.

"A Conductor" (picture 83) is also a relief (15 by 12 inches) modeled in clay, cast in plaster of Paris, and colored. After having been in the course for almost a year, with many interruptions caused by occupational pressures, Mr. W accomplished this work. The stiffness found in his earlier figures has given way to a more vital expression. It is still a modest work; but in view of his absolutely undeveloped beginning, this last achievement merits respect. It can be assumed that Mr. W, having found a natural basis for the development of his inherent artistic abilities, would have reached more complex stages if he had not been compelled by circumstances to withdraw from the course.

Chapter Six

THE EXPERIMENT WITH PERSONS IN BUSINESS AND THE PROFESSIONS

THE EXPERIMENT with persons in business and in the professions was begun in the summer of 1939 and was continued into the fall of 1943. During this period four persons participated: a broker, a social worker, a nursery-school teacher and a former college instructor. Their ages ranged from twenty-seven to fifty-four. The group met once each week for six months—until they felt able to work independently at home and bring their work in for discussion. The hours of work varied greatly in accordance with the pressures of their occupational and home activities, as well as with their desire to proceed. It is therefore difficult to establish the time during which they actively participated; but this is not essential, since the primary purpose of these reports is to show the natural unfolding and growth of their innate artistic abilities.

The development of Miss G. E., the social worker, is chosen to determine the experiment with this group.

Miss E was thirty-three when she entered the course. She has a master's degree in social work and is engaged in the medical-social field. American-born of Norwegian parents, she visited Norway several times—a fact which is mentioned in view of her choice of subjects, to be discussed later. Except for a brief period of superficial interest in art, at a time when she was influenced by association with an artist friend and took some drawing lessons, she had no training in this field. Of this experience she said: "We met once a week, drawing from a model one week and from still life the next. I did not do well, and when I dropped out after a short time I had no aspirations toward doing anything further with art." She said that her interest was rekindled when she heard that the author's approach to art had some social significance. She joined the course in the hope that she might be able to help others toward arts and crafts, as well as to find purposeful leisure-time activity for herself.

84. Miss E's first drawings.

At the first lesson, Miss E was told to "scribble" anything that might come to mind. Remarking that "people are my primary interest," she drew a few human figures, then suddenly changed to a different subject—cows. Asked what drawing she liked best, she unhesitatingly chose a cow and continued spontaneously to cover another sheet of paper with this object.

A close observation of the first sheet of drawings (picture 84) reveals that the cows appear in their total shape, showing the whole body with four legs, two ears, head, and tail. The intentional figure that carries the meaning, cow, is extended and directed in its principal characteristic according to a definite organization of form—the horizontal-vertical,—and the connection between tail and body already indicates the beginning of a transition to the stage of variability of direction of lines. This simple form represents the pictorial reflection of a definite stage of Miss E's visual conception.

The second series of drawings (picture 85) already brings out clearly the beginning of the stage of variability of direction of lines. Not only does the relationship of legs to body take over this new relationship, but the more differentiated outline of the head also substantiates a further differentiation. After finishing this sheet, Miss E said she "saw great need for improvement." She was requested to place her drawing at a distance and observe it for a

85. Miss E's second sheet of drawings.

while until she should get a new idea for improving it. In order to facilitate her visual judgment, it was suggested that she fill in with ink the outlines of some of the figures. As a result, the figure-ground relationship came more clearly into view and made visual judgment easier.

Miss E observed her drawings for about ten minutes, and then, with the remark, "I think I've got a better idea," went on with another drawing (picture 86). Upon completing it, she seemed satisfied, for she showed it to another participant in the course, a young broker. This drawing is a perfect example of the early artistic stage of the greatest contrast of direction, to which she regressed in order to attain the clearest visual idea of a cow. Her satisfaction in this result indicates the conformity between her visual comprehension and the work, through which regression to an earlier form becomes fully justified. The totality of form in this drawing must have had its origin in a visual conception that was based on a deep interest in the subject matter. When she was asked how she got the idea of drawing cows, Miss E told of her childhood experiences on a farm. She was requested to write down what she had said, and the following is her statement:

"You ask me to write of my interest in cows. As I think about this, I realize that I actually do have a very warm feeling for cows. As a child I lived for over a year on my grandfather's farm in Norway and my whole life at this time was centered in his fifty-two cows. I knew them all by name and my

86. In this drawing Miss E reaches a clearer visual conception of a cow, based on the primary stage of the greatest contrast of direction of lines.

greatest joy was to go with the Sweitzer and Burman, the dog, to fetch them home from the hills and woods for milking. Even now as I write I can easily recapture my love for them and the joy I felt when I was given a particular cow that I could milk every evening, and my pride when a newborn calf was named after me. I can see them all let out in the spring after their winter in the barn, jumping, running, almost dancing with the joy of being out in the open air again and feeling free to move their cramped limbs. I can see them on the hills grazing, I can hear their bells, I can see them lying or standing quietly under a tree, their faces and bodies expressions of repose and peace as they chewed and chewed. In fact my whole feeling concerning cows is one of peace, repose, and quiet beauty of green and brown hills with a church steeple and white farmhouse in the distance and the dark woods hemming in the quiet. For years my ambition in life was to return to Norway and become a farmer, and even now whenever I see cows or pass through rolling dairy country, I feel a wave of nostalgia. So perhaps it isn't so strange that I take this subject seriously and find pleasure in drawing cows."

87. Embroidery, "Pond with cows coming to it from all sides for water." (45 by 60 inches)

Miss E's impressive description of her life on a Norwegian farm reveals an abundance of deep-rooted visual experiences which have remained vital many years after their occurrence and have been purified of all unessential details. Such experiences sink into the subconscious, they are totally related to one's being, they are entirely humanized and form the best material for a visual conception. It is therefore understandable that Miss E was stimulated to draw further from the well of her childhood experiences for the subject matter of her pictures.

Her next drawing, which later was applied to an embroidery (picture 87), was of a pond with cows coming to it from all sides for water. She drew a circle for the pond in the center of the page, then lines running from it which were pathways. Since the cows were to approach the pond, she drew them facing inward on the pathway lines. In accordance with her then stage of visual conceiving, each path became a horizontal base line upon which the cows were vertically directed. In a manner analogous to that of the pictorial construction described in pictures 6 to 9, each path conditioned the relationship of the vertically directed cows. In each space between two paths on the border of the pond she placed a tree. Now, the outline of the round pond, which takes over the function of a base line, determines the vertically directed trees. The horizontal-vertical structure of form within the trees is also to be noted. In the organization of waves within the pond, too, one finds a definite order, the waves being placed in a relationship of direction to the outline of the pond.

As simple as it may appear, the embroidery demonstrates a well-organized visual formation that manifests an independent mental result of visual conceiving.

In order that substantiated reports on how the work affected the participants of the course might be obtained, they were requested to write brief statements from time to time. Miss E wrote, concerning the embroidery:

"So certain was I of my design that I did not lay it out on my material before I started, but evolved the pond, trees, and cows as I progressed. This was of course bad planning and led in part to the unevenness of my work. But that I received joy through doing it, that I found myself looking forward to an evening when I might pick it up again, that I had the feeling it was all my own—design as well as execution,—turned it into a thing well worth doing, and gave it its primary value. It has opened to me the possibility of many, many enjoyable evenings ahead—evenings of designing, drawing, embroidery intermixed for years to come."

While she worked on her embroidery at home, she drew, when taking her lessons, other pictures based on childhood experiences. "Taking the Cows Home from the Hill" (picture 88) is a picture that represents typical transition stages. Although most of the figures are clearly set off from their surrounding ground, the formation of the three hills indicates already the stage of the borderless transition from parts with figural meaning to parts with ground meaning. In effect, the hill in the middle gives the impression of being partly placed behind the two other hills. The fact that she did not emphasize the parts with figural or ground meaning by shading (see picture 14) points to her rather undeveloped ability of conceiving visually this problem of depth. Space is predominately determined by the figure-ground relationship of all the other objects; that is, figures are clearly organized above and below, and side by side, with respect to each other. Moreover, depth is further expressed by gradual diminution of the size of the objects from the lower to the upper

88. Drawing, "Taking the Cows Home from the Hill."

part of the drawing. In effect, the cows and the trees become smaller and smaller the more distant they are meant to be. This pictorial realization of space that makes visible even the most distant objects does not originate from conceptual rules of mathematical perspective, but is based upon spontaneous visual experience.

While the forms of the cows represent the stage of the greatest contrast of direction, the forms of the trees are already advanced to differentiated variability of direction of lines.

In the lower right-hand corner of this picture there appears a pond with fish, and directly attached to the outline of the pond are grass and flowers—evidence that the coherence of form seen in the previous picture still exists. But the position of the flowers and grass around the pond, and the position of the cows on the paths, are still controlled by their curved base lines, and so the picture as a whole does not yet present a unified relationship of direction.

The fact that different stages of development of visual conceiving appear in the same picture may seem to contradict the assertion that unity of form is an essential characteristic of any organically developing process of visual configuration; but the contradiction disappears if one considers such a picture

89. Drawing, "A Farm Scene."

as a phase in the total process of Miss E's artistic unfolding, rather than an isolated phenomenon. In visual configuration, just as in the process of "productive thinking," there is a constant transition from one level of conception to a higher one. On any of these levels one observes a consistent unity of form, but on the way from one level to the next, stages of transition usually appear.

Our analysis shows that the whole picture consists of different organized structures. Nevertheless, they are all the result of a mental digestion of visual experience into definite relationships of form, and not mere imitation of nature. The picture must therefore be recognized as Miss E's independent achievement. Her spontaneous remark that the figures behind the cows are "Hans, the Sweitzer, myself as a little girl, and Burman the dog," indicates her intimate connection with the subject matter.

Miss E's interest in representing life on a Norwegian farm continued. (Picture 89.) The variability of direction of form first achieved in the structure of trees in the preceding picture is now further applied in her drawings of chickens, roosters, and human figures. These objects attain the effect of movement. There is also a new formation of flowers and grass surrounding the pond, which are organized in a unity of direction indicating that flowers and grass, now in conformity with the trees, grow upward. This, together with the extended application of variability of direction, adds essential elements toward a greater uniformity in this picture as compared with the preceeding one.

Miss E again turned her attention to cows. Before proceeding further with this subject, she was advised to judge her former drawings at length. "I begin to realize that my cows are very, very simple and naïve," she concluded, "and I am going to work at it until I get one that pleases me more." This led to a series of drawings which culminated in one that gave her "complete satisfaction in the feeling that I have perfected the cow as far as I can."

Satisfied with the new form which she had given her subject, she wanted to incorporate it into a theme. She recalled her drawing, "Taking the Cows Home from the Hill," and said that she wanted to repeat the theme, since she felt that she could now do it much better. On a standard sheet of typewriter paper she started a new drawing and in place of the three hills made only one. As she no longer liked the way she had drawn the cows coming downhill because they "appeared at such awkward angles," she worked out a new arrangement. When she had completed the new drawing of her former theme, she expressed pleasure over it. It was then suggested to her that she make it as a painting-on-cloth, to be used as a wall hanging.

This wall hanging (picture 90) marks an essential step in Miss E's artistic development. The whole picture—even its border—shows clearly the application of the stage of variability of direction, through which a considerable change in the forms of the cows had been attained. Their outlines show various curves and oscillations that take away from the bodies their stiffness and clumsiness. In comparison with the cows in the previous picture, which look as if they were drawn "upside down," they are now organized in a unified relationship of direction together with all the other figures. With respect to this change, Miss E writes: "No longer wishing to see the cows coming downhill at such awkward angles, I had to draw a serpentine pathway which gave me the opportunity of placing all the cows right side up."

90. Wall hanging painted on cloth, "Cows Coming Home from the Hills."
(54 by 33 inches)

As this statement reveals, the construction of the special pathway is not a result of deliberate imitation of nature, but is conditioned by the desire for an easier visual comprehension of the whole herd of cows: Therefore, they had to be organized in a unified relationship of direction. The same construction of form can be found in numberless works of folk art as well as in many representations of parades in engravings of the sixteenth and seventeenth centuries.

The wall hanging, as already mentioned, had its origin in a smaller drawing. The specific structure and decorative charm of the drawing led to the idea of applying it to a larger design. In other words, the drawing was not intentionally done in order to enlarge it for application to a wall hanging. Its particular artistic form, a result of a definite stage of visual conceiving, offered the possibility of creating a work of applied art. This example shows that in the development of one's inherent artistic potentialities the achievement of a work of applied art is the natural outcome of a definite stage of visual conception, rather than the product of a separate discipline and conscious effort to "design."

The completed wall hanging found its place in Miss E's home. She expressed its meaning to her as follows: "When I hung my painting-on-cloth on the wall, it set up the whole room and gave it more than a mere colorful decoration to me. It made the room more distinctly mine. When I returned home at night it even seemed to give me a feeling of welcome—a part of childhood that had come to life again. My friends all reacted to it spontaneously when they entered the room. Some thought it a good design, others thought it unique, and some felt it exceedingly naïve, but I always managed to sense a degree of approval which pleased me, even if it were only to laugh at the 'happy expression of the cows'. However, seeing my wall hanging daily, I began to note a need for still further improvement in the form of the cows, which appeared too flat to me. For example, I wanted to draw the legs so that I could distinguish the ones on the near side from those on the far side."

Miss E decided to improve the shape of her cows. Since she found them "too flat," improvement evidently meant emphasis on a certain roundness. To express roundness and depth among the parts by drawing, she would have had to model the whole body as well as its parts by applying dark tones at their borders. As this would have required an entirely new process of visual conceiving, and as she probably would have faced some difficulties, it was suggested that she make a relief of her cow by cutting it out of a plate of plaster of Paris. This change of medium served to facilitate the achievement of her new form. Drawing with pencil is governed solely by visual experience, but modeling or cutting out demands tactile experience as well. Furthermore, since the cutting-out process is naturally slower than drawing, it allows more

91. Painted relief in plaster of Paris. (13 by 17 inches)

time for critical observation. Hence it becomes understandable that where greater experience of the senses may contribute to an easier and clearer visual comprehension the shifting from drawing to sculpturing can be of great significance. The change of material in Miss E's next work was determined by purely pedagogical reasons in order that she might reach a clear artistic conception.

Miss E, like the other participants of the group, was requested to observe each step of the work in progress and to write down all essential phases. The following statement reveals her experience during the making of the relief in plaster of Paris (picture 91).

"The suggestion given me to cut a cow out of a plate of plaster of Paris stimulated a new interest in me, as I had never before used that material. The chiseling-out process was all-absorbing. Having to be exceedingly careful not to cut too deeply, I had to concentrate harder and proceed more slowly, which gave me a better opportunity to criticize my work. In addition to seeing what I was doing, I could also feel it with my fingers. Any harsh edge or rough curve that might escape my eye, my fingers would catch, and it gave me tactile pleasure to feel the smooth roundness of the borders and curves of the cow down the head and neck, over the shoulder hump, down the sway in the back, and up over the hips. I particularly enjoyed rounding the stomach, for not only could I make it curved the way I did in my drawings, but I could also round it from the bottom upward. The head was the most difficult, for I had to separate the ear and horn on the near side from the ones on the far side by a gradual series of depths. The legs presented the same difficulty, but when I cut them out the whole animal suddenly acquired a certain depth—a near side and a far side. I was also able to make the upper leg merge into the body rather than extend it from the body, as in my drawings, by cutting deeper that part of the body touching the upper legs. When the work was finished, I decided the relief would be more effective if I colored the cow so that it could stand out more clearly against the white plaster background. Now, colored in red-brown, I feel that the cow stands rounded and complete in relief. Though the cow is standing, it appears alive. There seems to be move-ment in the curves themselves, and these curves which I developed equally over the whole body to form the cow, together with the depth and roundness which I also tried to make equal, have given it life."

This report, as well as the relief itself, indicates progress in the achievement of a more complex configuration. In Miss E's earlier pictures, cows appeared flat: the original intentional figure had been extended in accordance with the stage of variability of direction, and the extended parts, the legs, had in turn been directed in an orderly manner. Now, by setting the far-side legs off from the near-side legs and the upper near-side legs from the body before they merge into it, the whole figure "suddenly acquired a certain depth." Close observation reveals that by cutting deeper into that part of the body which touches the upper near-side legs, the figural meaning of the upper near-side legs and the ground meaning of the adjacent body parts have been empha-sized: the whole body, which previously had only figural meaning, now has in some of its parts ground meaning for the neighboring figures, the upper near-side legs. The effect of depth is the result of the application of the stage of borderless transition from parts with figural meaning to parts with ground meaning. The same principle of form has been applied in the relationship of the far-side legs to the body. The outlined parts of the far-side legs carry figural meaning, but where they touch their adjacent figures they obtain ground meaning with respect to those figures. Furthermore, the same principle of form exists also in the relationship of the head to the body and of the ears and horns to the head. Thus, the total control of this stage of visual conceiving throughout the figure creates a more complex wholeness of form. It seems worth while to stress the fact that the necessity for the realization of this more differentiated stage of visual conceiving was rooted in Miss E's need for "further improvement of the forms of the cows." Her spontaneous step forward in the reaching of a more differentiated stage was based, therefore, upon an inner compulsion which became the underlying drive for her development. Miss E's statement, "these curves which I developed equally over the whole body to form the cow, together with the depth and roundness which I also tried to make equal, have given it life," indicates that she is on the way to experience genuine artistic activity in her creating of a unified wholeness of form by means of which "lifelike" qualities are pictorially realizable.

Picture 92 is a painting in tempera called "Farmer and Wife with Their Cow." Miss E, stimulated by another participant of the group who was painting in tempera, spontaneously designed and carried out this picture in that medium in one afternoon.

The representation of the cow reveals clearly the effect of the previous work upon Miss E's visual conceiving. Having achieved the relief of the cow in plaster of Paris by tactile as well as visual experience, she received so definite an idea of this new stage of visual conceiving that she was able to realize it also on canvas, that is, on a two-dimensional plane: she succeeded in her original intention of showing roundness and depth in the cow.

All figures, man, cow, woman, and tree, are placed upon the upper border of the path. Thus, the figures by receiving a horizontal base line produce an impression of standing on a ground. The path itself, with its stones of different size and color, appears in utmost clearness. The direction of the path, parallel to the border of the canvas, finds repetition in the upper border of the field that forms the horizon, as well as in the horizontal base lines for the haystacks.

This means that the main structure of this picture is built upon the early stage of the greatest contrast of direction of lines. In spite of already having reached the stage of the borderless transition, as is shown in the overlappings within the forms of the cow and the human beings, Miss E utilizes an earlier stage of visual conception in the principal structure in order to obtain a clear

92. "Farmer and Wife with Their Cow," a painting in tempera. (16 by 20 inches)

perceptual grasp of the total theme. This structure is supported by a distinct figure-ground relationship between human beings, cow, and tree as figures, and field and sky as ground. The plain colors of the objects still emphasize this structure. Overlapping of cow and tree trunk is convincingly expressed by the light brown body of the cow and the black trunk. In order to make the head of the woman best visible against the light field, it was intentionally outlined by a dark contour. Concerning the form of the haystacks, Miss E states: "The haystacks were a bit difficult, for it was impossible to draw the many individual straws, but then it occurred to me to make outlines for the stacks and paint some individual straws within their borders." The multiplicity of the shapes in a haystack demanded regression to the primitive stage of the "intentional figure" outlined and directed. Only in this way could they become visually comprehensible.

In summary, the organization of this picture gives a definite meaning to all its parts. Nothing has been done arbitrarily. Throughout the whole picture, visual thought is manifested; and, with it, originality. The meaning of this work—which presents a typical transition stage—can only be understood in the sequence of further development of Miss E's artistic abilities.

Encouraged by her first painting, Miss E decided to make a large one to which she intended to devote several weeks. It is impossible to show here all the drawings of cows, horses, wagons, trees, and persons that led up to the picture, "Bringing Home the Hay" (picture 93).

Compared with the preceding painting, this one displays the same pictorial organization in its main structure: again all the base lines—for the horse, wagon, men, trees, cows, grass, and hills—run parallel to the lower border of the canvas. All figures are in a unity of direction to one another whereby the total picture becomes easily grasped. Even on the basis of this comparatively simple structure, the figures obtain a greater complexity of form convincingly expressed in the more differentiated stage of variability of direction in trees, human beings, and cows, than in the previous painting. In other words, a definite cognition of form that was previously reached has been applied in a more differentiated way to a larger number of figures. In effect, the picture receives a greater expression of movement and vitality. Similarly, the stage of the borderless transition whereby the forms of cows are given a certain roundness and depth is also extended to the form of a horse. In the formation of the hills the borderless transition exists also, but in a still earlier state, "back and forth" being demonstrated by a discrimination of greens—dark green for near-side hills and light green for far-side hills.

Attention may be directed to the way in which the mass of hay on the wagon is realized. Miss E gives her own explanation for this particular form: "I knew exactly how to draw the wagon of hay, as I had made several sketches and discovered that the only way I could do it without getting a chaotic mass of straws was to make a clear outline of a load of hay filled in with brown and then paint the individual straws in yellow to give the brown mass meaning." In other words, this highly differentiated object was difficult to grasp visually.

In order to avoid confusion she again regressed to a much earlier stage of visual conception in simplifying the mass of hay to an "outlined intentional figure," and within this figure she placed the individual straws side by side, each one of them being distinctly set off from its ground. Only by means of this formation was she able to grasp the mass of hay as a whole. Regression to so primitive a stage was, therefore, an indispensable necessity.

93. "Bringing Home the Hay," a painting in tempera. (22 by 28 inches)

In another part of this picture there is an additional illustration of the need for gaining visual clearness by the application of an early stage of visual conceiving. "When I thought the picture was finished," Miss E wrote, "I found that the green of the pasture did not look like a pasture, so I filled it in with dark green grass. But then I discovered that the cows and grass did not seem to be standing on the ground, and therefore I drew a dark line under each object to fasten it down. With respect to this, I should perhaps mention that I was later surprised to be shown a book of East Indian miniatures of the seventeenth century in which I found several pictures with lines drawn under the figures. One in particular that caught my attention was a picture of a polo game in which there was a dark line under each human figure, horse, and grass stalk. Before having discovered in the painting of my picture that a line was essential to keep the grass and cows from floating, I would probably have surmised that these dark lines were intended as shadows. But now I rather imagine that the artist might have felt as I did that the lines kept his figures too from floating, and somehow this recognition of art-forms through my own experience was of particular interest to me."

Although the whole picture still represents a transition stage, it is evident that each particular structure is the result of a definite way of visual conceiving and that the formation of trees, human beings, and cows manifests a change toward a configuration of a more complex form.

Months had passed since Miss E had joined the experimental group. She always showed great interest and revealed remarkable perseverance in the achievement of her aims. Her personal gain from the course is summed up in her own words: "Several months have passed since my last report and I feel that every gain made up to that point has been increased. The work continues to be a very great source of recreational pleasure to me which stands far above any I have ever engaged in. I look forward to an undisturbed evening of painting with a joy that actually fills my whole being and is reflected even in my daily activities. In fact, life itself is more satisfying with this all-absorbing interest to turn to at the end of the day, especially when I have that good feeling that my day's work has entitled me to indulge fully in it."

Miss E planned the following work (picture 94) immediately after completing the preceding one. "I want to show still more," she said. "I want to show my grandfather's farm with the apple orchard around it and the hay-field adjoining it, and to make the hills, which were so important to that setting, more distinct."

Through concentrated work in the achievement of her earlier pictures, each one of which was realized according to her maximum artistic abilities, Miss E's visual conceiving was so strengthened that she was now able to design directly on canvas without any preparatory drawings. The cultivation of this mental process is not dependent on pictorial productions alone, but is also decisively fostered by visual imagery. This was especially true in Miss E's case because, on account of her daily occupation, she was able to devote only occasional evenings to painting. This is made clear in her own observations: "At odd times during the day, on my way to and from work or in quiet moments at the office, I found myself thinking of my picture and how I would paint it. I was also conscious of being aware of things I had hardly noticed before. I was surprised, for example, to discover that there were many more horses on the street than I had realized—horses drawing varied types of wagons such as are used for hauling vegetables, milk, rags and iron, flowers,

94. "My Grandfather's Farm," a painting in oils. (22 by 28 inches)

groceries, and moving vans—and I observed them all. I observed trees too and looked long at each one I passed. The horses and trees always brought me back to my picture, or perhaps my picture brought the horses and trees to my attention, but in either case my observations enriched my ideas and gradually the picture became clearer in my mind."

This statement points to an essential factor within this art-educational procedure. Observers of these experiments have often wondered how students could develop their artistic abilities to more complex forms without being confronted with objects of nature. Miss E's report may in some degree elucidate this problem. While she was "thinking" of her picture, she became more "conscious" of the world of things around her. Her urge for a clear visual comprehension of the subject matter led her spontaneously to an intent observation of nature. Thus, things became intimately related to her. A vital interest, an irresistible compulsion to grasp those objects visually, to take mental possession of them, was the underlying drive for her approach to the visible world. With her growing artistic abilities, things became of greater significance to her, and she drew from nature what she needed for the building of her mental world, the world of her visual conception.

Compared with all her previous pictures, this one indicates immediately a great difference in its main structure. A stone wall, starting at the left on the lower border of the canvas, runs slantwise through the entire plain to the horizontal base line upon which the hills are resting. Thus, the wall divides the plain into a green apple orchard at the left and a light yellow field at the right. This new structure can only be explained by another application of the stage of variability of direction of lines. The long stone wall, which gradually becomes smaller the closer it approaches the hills, emphasizes the large extension of the plain and determines in the formation of the field the gradual diminution of the haystacks, a diminution which in turn points to the far distance of the hills as well as to the vast plain. But the greatest effect of the extended application of the stage of variability of direction has been reached in the figures of the working farmers. Her mastery and application of the stage of variability of direction enabled her to impart to the human figures an aspect of motion. Further progress can be noted in the formation of the hills. Through the use of stronger colors—dark green, light green, yellow-green, and yellow—a greater distinction of "back and forth" has been accomplished. All other objects still show the same structural qualities as those in the preceding painting, but the fact that she could utilize them for the pictorial upbuilding of a new picture may throw some light on the increased unfolding in the organization of creative energies.

While Miss E was painting the two farmers haying, she became so absorbed in the subject matter that she decided to make a special picture with this theme. It should first of all be noted that this picture (picture 95) shows a harmonious expression of movement not only in the human figures but also in the formation of the entire earth ground, including the wheatstacks. This means that for the first time in Miss E's artistic activity the stage of variability of direction of lines is realized in the total pictorial structure. Moreover, spatial depth is also harmoniously organized over the whole painting by the application of the stage of the borderless transition from figural to ground meaning. For example, the earth formation on which the taller farmer is standing starts at the lower border of the canvas with light yellow and grows

95. "Farmers Haying," a painting in tempera. (16 by 20 inches)

gradually darker toward its upper border, where its figural meaning is clearly brought out by a light yellow of the adjacent earth formation that carries ground meaning. The same principle of form is applied to all the other earth formations, including the hills which are farther back. It can also be observed within the forms of the human figures in the overlappings of upper arms and chest, of upper legs, and of face and neck. It should be pointed out, too, that the stage of the borderless transition is here realized by color nuances, which means that this picture, compared with all Miss E's previous ones, reveals a much more differentiated sense for total coloration, a harmony in the relationships of color nuances. In sum: through the total application of the stage of variability of direction of lines, together with the stage of the borderless transition, the whole picture receives a complete unity of form.

If one looks back at the pictorial configurations of Miss E's earlier works, it may become obvious that each one prepares step by step for the present visual synthesis of form. A just evaluation of these pictures, therefore, can only be undertaken by considering them within the proper sequence of Miss E's artistic development, for only then do they obtain their meaning as indispensable milestones on the way toward the present pictorial achievement. The structures of the previous pictures mark the organic growth of Miss E's artistic ability because each one of them determines thoroughly the ground for the new pictorial organization of the following one.

The theme of the next picture has its origin in another childhood experience, which Miss E describes as follows: "While I was drawing scenes from my early recollections, an experience with a lost cow came vividly to mind. Our summer neighbor, in a Wisconsin village, had an only cow which grazed on the edge of the woods near our home. One day the cow had strayed into the woods and her mistress gave my cousin and me each twenty-five cents to look for her. This was big money and adventure to us, all in one, and we started off in high spirits. But within an hour we, too, were lost in those dark woods. Tired, homesick, and very frightened, we sat down on a log to rest. There was silence everywhere. No sounds came in from the outside world. Then suddenly we heard a faint tinkle of a bell. As we eagerly listened, we heard it again. Renewed in spirits we followed the tinkle, which gradually sounded nearer and nearer until at last we came face to face with our cow. We were so glad to meet this other lost soul, whose calm expression and dark eyes were somehow reassuring that we hugged her with joy. She immediately started walking slowly and carefully over the underbrush and between trees while we followed confident in the feeling that we were safe again. Soon she led us to a path and from there directly home."

In this painting, called "Cow Lost in the Woods" (picture 96), the structure of the earth—determined by the same principle of form as seen in the previous picture—has been most clearly worked out. The colors of the grass, bushes, and leaves on the ground are determined by this structure. For instance, on top of each dark earth formation, grass and bushes had to be painted in dark green in order to be set off from their light ground. The same was necessary for the leaves, which had to be light on a dark ground and vice versa. That is to say, the different colors of the earth ground, as well as those of all parts belonging to it, are conditioned by a definite construction of form—the borderless transition from parts with figural meaning to parts with ground meaning. The peculiar shapes of the trees indicate a regression to an earlier stage

96. "Cow Lost in the Woods," a painting in oils. (16 by 20 inches)

of visual conceiving. (See picture II.) The reason for such a regression becomes evident through Miss E's description of the process of reaching these forms: "I found the woods exceedingly difficult to paint. I started off well enough, but when it came to the branches and leaves overlapping with the branches and leaves of other trees, I achieved nothing but confusion. I could no longer distinguish to which trees the branches belonged or to which branches the leaves were attached. I tried over and over again, attempting to differentiate the trees, branches, and leaves by different colors and different-shaped leaves, but I always ended in the same confused mass at the points of overlapping.

Finally, after a long and sustained effort to achieve clarity, it occurred to me to enclose the branches and leaves of each tree into an outlined treetop form. I colored each treetop with a shade of green that would distinguish one tree from the other. Then I painted the branches and leaves within the boundaries of the outlines. In the trees with the lighter green enclosures I had to paint dark leaves in order to show them clearly, while in the back tree with the dark enclosure I had to paint light leaves. This removed all confusion and solved for me the problem of the overlapping of the trees."

Miss E's report clearly points out that the regression in the forms of her trees to an earlier stage of visual conceiving was a necessity for reaching "clarity." By giving the branches and leaves within each outlined tree a distinct figure-ground relationship, and by making the enclosure of the rear tree dark and that of the front trees light, she attained a clear visual comprehension of this complicated problem. In solving "the problem of the overlapping of the trees" she had applied the stage of borderless transition, as is shown in the structure of the form of the earth ground as well as in that of the cow. This means that a pictorial organization previously achieved conditioned the configuration of a new pictorial task. Therewith it becomes obvious that the principle of organic growth is the underlying force of Miss E's creative unfolding of inherent artistic abilities.

Thus far, Miss E's themes revolve around one principal interest, farm life. This particular interest, this certain love of the subject of her experience, enabled her at the beginning of her pictorial activity to conceive visually a cow in a simple, unified form. Gradually she extended her interest in such a way that one subject matter led to the next. This fact may throw some light upon the significance which the discovery of one's innermost interest may have upon one's artistic growth. Even the simplest drawing, as long as it is the result of visual conceiving, always points to the producer's intimate relation to the subject of his representation. It is this innermost connection between subject matter and artistic form which assures an organic unfolding of one's inherent artistic abilities.

A few days after the completion of the picture we have just discussed, Miss E had an experience which was of great importance to her artistic development. "I sat across the subway aisle from a young, stunning-looking Negress," she wrote, "whose clear features were so striking that I found myself staring at her. Her face was wholly negroid—black eyes, wide nostrils, full lips, and a coloring of beautiful brown. She was dressed up in finery with necklace, bracelets, and rings, but as she sat there with her arms folded in her lap she gave the impression of great simplicity. I was so fascinated by her that on reaching home I immediately tried to draw her. For the first time in my life I felt that I had so clear an image of a person that I could paint her."

Before she started to paint the Negress, Miss E did two small preparatory drawings which showed already the essential features of a Negro woman as she described them in her report. Encouraged by these convincing results, she chose a canvas of 30 by 25 inches for her painting. During her entire execution of the work she displayed a definite determination to unify lines and colors in the structure of her picture. It became evident that she harbored in her mind a clear idea about her subject matter. The monumental effect of the finished picture (picture 97) rests mainly upon the pictorial realization of a distinct figure-ground relationship of all parts. The entire background was painted in a blue-green that sets off strongly the black hair, the brown head, the upper arms, and especially the light red dress and the yellow wicker bench. The light red dress in turn creates an excellent ground meaning for the dark brown arms placed on it. Simple color nuances can be found only in the face, where the nose is brought out by darker surrounding areas. The upper part of the neck is also darkened in order to distinguish the neck from the head, and slight color nuances are found under the breasts to indicate their roundness. In the relationship of these parts Miss E attempted to apply the stage of the borderless transition. To apply this principle of form over the whole body did not occur to her. Without ever mentioning the problem of the borderless transition, she accomplished the picture as it is. She avoided any complication by realizing the whole body through the stage of the "intentional figure extended and directed" in a definite way. By a broadening of the intentional figure at the hips, a sitting position was realized. That is, she attained a visual comprehension of the whole body by regressing to an earlier stage of visual conceiving. This powerful painting could only be achieved through the fact that the clear and simple features of the natural object which were instantly grasped by her enabled her to transform immediately her visual experience into a visually comprehensible image. She reached that rare state in which the artist and the world become one.

For the next painting Miss E's own statement may serve as an introduction. "During my painting of the 'Negro Woman' I found myself more and

97. "Negro Woman," an oil painting. (30 by 25 inches)

more drawn to our colored patients at the hospital in which I work. I became increasingly aware that many more of them possessed great beauty than I had previously realized. They presented a new interest to me and I fear that during some interviews I must actually have appeared rude as my attention shifted from their eyes to each single feature—eyebrows, nose, lips, shape of face, hair. When I saw the three-year-old son of one of these patients holding tight to the clinic bench on which he was sitting, I had to stop long to look at him, for I knew this was something I wanted to hold in mind. With his very large eyes and perfect, small, negroid features he seemed somehow a wholly complete little being. The same evening I started my first draft, and I have worked it over several times until now I have completed a painting of him sitting—not in our hospital setting, but on a rock in Morningside Park with Harlem in the background.''

The accomplishment of this painting, which measures 30 by 25 inches (picture 98), required several weeks of hard work. Each new form was carefully prepared through special drawings, and hence, when the process of painting began, Miss E faced no essential difficulties. In spite of its greater complexity this picture signifies immediately that the powerful expression of the preceding painting has been maintained. Through the emphasis on the boy his figure embodies the principal meaning of the whole picture. This effect is intensified by the sharp contrast between the figure and the background. The contrast is produced by the figure-ground relationship of the dark brown head against the light yellow-green evening sky, by the white shirt against the dark reddish-brown complex of the houses, by the intensely red shorts against the light gray surface of the rocks on which the boy is sitting, and finally, by the dark brown legs, red stockings, and black shoes against the light gray side view of the rock.

It should be noted that Miss E conceived this picture in such a way that the main subject, the Negro boy, is set off against a background by means of his large size and central position and by the contrast of brightness and color. The application of the structural principle at which Miss E arrived in this painting is not limited to the visual arts. It is, for instance, commonly used in music when a main theme is made to stand out against the accompaniment by means of louder sound, use of different instruments, or distinctions of melodic structure. This is one of the numerous examples which can be given to illustrate the thesis that order and expression are obtained in pictorial work

98. "Negro Boy Sitting in Morningside Park, with Harlem in the Background,"
an oil painting. (30 by 25 inches)

through general organizational principles which are found in other productive activities of the human mind.

Besides the formation of the boy's figure as the governing theme of this picture, there are newly attained values of form which point to an essential enrichment of Miss E's artistic conception.

In this painting rocks appear for the first time. Their form apparently displays a complicated way of visual conceiving, because they have been realized so that their surfaces and both front and side views are visible. However, a close observation reveals that their structure is of a simple kind used in a relatively complicated way. Vertical lines—representing front and side edges of the rock—are connected at their tops to other lines at various angles, a means by which the upper edges are extended to the right and left and then turn toward and meet each other again. Thus, they shape the surface of the rocks. This means that the structure of the rocks is based upon a new application of the stage of variability of direction of lines (as demonstrated in picture 13). By coloring the surface a light gray and the different front and side views darker grays, each rock has been made to take on a spatial appearance. This structural formation determined the sitting position of the boy. His upper legs are in a relationship of direction to the right-hand part of the surface of the rock, while his lower legs run parallel to the vertical front edges.

The form of trees in all the preceding pictures is marked by the stage of variability of direction of lines: branches and leaves are distinctly set off from their background and do not interfere with one another. In this painting the stage of borderless transition, as seen in the formation of the earth ground, and previously in the relationships of the trees in picture 96, now becomes the governing principle for the formation of the bush and of all trees. Thus a certain appearance of spatial depth between leaves and sections of leaves was achieved. This principle of form appears further in the overlappings of the various rocks, and in the figure of the boy where it brings out the head from the neck, creates the formation of the folds in the white shirt, and the overlapping of the shorts on the upper legs.

The fact that a relatively complicated principle of form, such as the stage of borderless transition from parts with figural meaning to parts with ground meaning, could be applied all over the picture, has created an artistic organization on a comparatively high level. The attainment of this result required Miss E's entire efforts and so was of particular value to her. This is evident through her own statement: "Of all my paintings so far, this one of the Negro boy has given me the greatest satisfaction. The others represented a thoroughly enjoyable hobby which was to me the main object of painting, but as I worked on this picture I grew increasingly aware that a new note had been added. It wasn't only fun, by any means. It was hard, very hard work. For weeks I struggled with problems—getting a sitting position for the boy, the making of rocks, the bush in the foreground, the trees, the houses, and with all these the main problem of keeping the boy the central interest. I wanted, for example, to achieve space in the bush, but this was difficult to work out. However, when I stressed space between the leaves by darkening the underleaves at the points of overlappings, I was able to do the same with the whole bush by dividing it into sections and darkening these too at the points of overlappings. The one bush—in fact, the first overlapping of leaves in that bush—set the formation of all the leaves and all the trees. Once started, there was no other choice but to carry it all out in this particular way, and to do it required sustained concentration. But the very fact that it was not easy and that it was a wholehearted venture to which I gave many an evening of my entire attention and energy, made it for me a thing of accomplishment.

"One evening, working long past midnight on one tree alone, I began to wonder why I was allowing myself to spend so much time and energy on it, why I couldn't call it quits and go to bed and why this was such an often-repeated procedure. I knew I would scold myself the next morning, yet I couldn't stop. I had to complete what I started, for I couldn't judge the whole tree before it was finished, nor see its effect on the rest of the picture. The high moments in working always come when I stand back to see how the newly painted object takes its place in the whole picture. If it harmonizes well with the other objects and its effect brings further life to the picture, then I can go to bed happy. If, however, it does not harmonize with the other objects, then I can at least wipe it out before the paint dries and save the painting from ruin. Fortunately, wasted efforts of this type occur less and less frequently, for I plan my work as a whole much better now. I wish I could say the same concerning my other interests, for it has always been my nature to plunge hastily into activity without clear thought or organization, but only in painting have I been conscious of suffering the consequences. I have had to take care, had to organize, had to have a clear idea and to work it out with regard to complete perfection or nothing would come of it."

Miss E's statement brings out in a bold way the great difference between uncontrolled "self-expression," recreational fun or play alone, and play in a higher sense disciplined by severe intellectual effort. The unfolding of organized energies in the artistic process and its effect upon the personality are here clearly noted.

Miss E speaks about having to have "a clear idea and to work it out with regard to complete perfection or nothing would come of it." To many observers of the picture of the Negro boy her concept of "complete perfection" might seem questionable. From a naturalistic viewpoint—and this is commonly the yardstick of judgment of the usual observer—this painting may be far removed from any "perfection." However, a just evaluation of this work can only be undertaken by considering it as the pictorial realization of a particular stage of Miss E's visual conception. The complete working-out of her idea of space in all the objects of this painting is her "perfection." "The perfection of the object is something of which the critic cannot judge, its beauty something that he cannot feel, if he has not like the original artist made himself such as the thing itself should be. . . . The 'appreciation of art' must not be confused with the psychoanalysis of our likes and dislikes, dignified by the name of 'aesthetic reaction.'"[1] A just comprehension and evaluation of a work of art presupposes "a bringing to life in ourselves of the form in which the artist conceived the work and by which he judged it."[2]

Miss E returned to her recollections of Norway for her next theme (picture 99). "Now that I am able to paint rocks, I want to draw a mountain scene. I often recall the ecstasy I experienced when, again in Norway, at the age of eighteen, I stood on a mountaintop for the first time in my life and looked out at the panorama of mountain ranges below and beyond. It was one of those supreme moments in life when one feels with all one's being, yet is never able to recapture it in words. I would like to express that feeling I had of being, so to say, on top of the world looking down, and I have chosen the mountain goat, which to my mind belongs in this setting, as the essential object around which to paint the picture."

Later, Miss E adds this illuminating account of the development of this work: "In working out the relationship of the foreground mountaintop to the mountains below and beyond, I found myself so interested in doing this task

[1] Ananda K. Coomaraswamy, *The Christian and Oriental or True Philosophy of Art* (John Stevens, 29 Thames Street, Rhode Island, 1939), p. 9.
[2] *Ibid.*

99. "Mountain Goat Looking Out on Mountain Ranges Below and Beyond,"
an oil painting. (24 by 20 inches)

that it became my chief concern. In fact, I became so excited in working this out, using dark to bring out the light foreground, and vice versa, that I almost forgot my theme. It was the first time that the form itself had become such a source of interest, and strange as it may seem I had never reached the same degree of excitement when my major interest was in the contents."

These words reveal the state in which the artist reaches the heights of his mental activity—the activity of creative formation. The content of representation has almost disappeared: principal concentration is given to that mental process through which the content obtains form, that is, its artistic existence. The comprehension of this process through one's own experience is of great importance. Not only does it open an insight into the essence of one's own artistic activity, but simultaneously—as will be demonstrated later—it also makes possible an understanding of other works of art which reflect a similar stage of artistic configuration.

This painting, like the preceding one, required many preparatory drawings. It also presents, like the preceding one, a central theme. The striking effect of this object is again accomplished by a distinct figure-ground relationship—a white goat against a reddish sky. In spite of the overlappings of legs the whole figure is convincingly visualized. In the same way that the outlines of each pair of legs diverge upward, so do the corresponding contours of the whole figure. The upward direction of all these outlines finds its end in the vertically directed oscillating line of the back. This structure gives to the total figure a unified organization of form based upon an orderly application of the stage of variability of direction of lines, by means of which, in turn, the whole attains a certain tension and vitality. Variability of direction of lines and unified relationship of direction of lines govern the construction of mountains as well as of rocks. Whereas the rocks in the preceding picture are simply placed, one behind another, without great differences in their colors—a lack of difference which causes the whole painting to remain relatively flat,—this painting shows a strong emphasis of difference between light foreground and dark background without giving up its great decorative quality. The spatial depth has been achieved by stressing the borderless transition from background to foreground through the strongest distinctions of light and dark. Furthermore, the foreground and the background contain in themselves the stage of borderless transition in their separate parts; for example, the dark near side of the foreground passes borderless over into the

100. "A Norwegian Fjord," a pencil drawing. (19½ by 11½ inches)

light far side of the foreground. This means that the stage of borderless transition from parts with figural meaning to parts with ground meaning, which had appeared already in the spatial structure of the goat, has been applied in an extended manner to the spatial structure of the whole picture. And thus the painting becomes a unified order of form.

The drawing, "A Norwegian Fjord" (picture 100), shows still further application of the stage of visual conceiving just discussed; instead of only foreground and background, three mountain ranges are pictorially organized behind one another. The attainment of this complicated configuration of form required eleven preceding studies, each of which was carried to partial completion. After thorough visual judgment of each of those studies, new, more integrated pictorial formations were conceived, until the artistic form of this drawing fully satisfied Miss E—an indication that it became the best achievement she was able to create.

The more complicated ideas of spatial depth, combined with the highly differentiated stage of variability of direction of lines demonstrated in the last two pictures, marks a culmination of successive artistic efforts. The structures of all previous pictures led gradually to this point. In other words, each preceding artistic stage prepared thoroughly for the formation of each succeeding one up to the present level of development. This means that the progress of Miss E's work rests on a natural organic growth of her artistic abilities. Although the picture of a Norwegian fjord is her latest one at the time this report is submitted, she shows every indication of continuing her work. Her case reveals to what unexpected degree of genuine artistic performance a layman can advance if his abilities are unfolded in accordance with inherent evolutionary processes of visual conceiving. The formative effect which the awakening of such unknown creative potentialities has had upon Miss E's personality has been formulated at various stages of her work by herself. The enrichment which her creative activity means to her, especially in her approaches to artistic works of others, is disclosed in the following statement about visits to the Metropolitan Museum of Art in New York.

"My powers of observation are definitely increasing in that I am far more aware of what I see than I previously was, and with this, fortunately, my ability to enjoy and appreciate the works of others has also grown. I say fortunately, for I have actually disliked looking at pictures in museums and art galleries. Ever since childhood, when I was on occasion brought to the Art

Institute of Chicago, I have developed a backache shortly after starting the rounds in any museum and my discomfort increased with the years, particularly when in the presence of one possessing a knowledge of art. Though a subject matter here and there held my attention, never did a picture stir me enough to pull me back to any museum or gallery for another glimpse. I regret having to confess this complete lack of appreciation and great gap in my education, but from the viewpoint of evaluating the meaning of this course to me, I must explain that I brought to it no appreciation or understanding of art whatsoever.

"Now, however, I can say that I have not only spent an afternoon in the Metropolitan Museum of Art without developing a backache, but of late I have even returned many times alone and of my own volition. This change dates back to a Sunday afternoon when I was taken directly to the room of the Early Italian paintings and left alone to observe them. At first I walked around the room in my usual museum manner, staring blankly from one painting to the other, moving closer to some every now and again pretending intelligent interest—and then I was through. As I was to spend at least an hour there, I relaxed on a bench in the middle of the room and watched the people passing by—many of whom did not even pretend to look at the pictures, or assumed attitudes so closely related to mine that they irritated me. One man, however, stood for a long, long time before a painting, took out his magnifying glass and studied it, then stepped back to observe it and was so absorbed that others like myself gathered to see what he was looking at, and, not seeing, moved on. Finally I stood before a crucifixion painting in a corner of the room. As I stared at it for the second time, some rocks in the foreground of that picture suddenly awakened an interest in me. They looked familiar. I leaned closer and saw that they were painted in a similar way to mine. This was a fascinating discovery: I had painted rocks in the manner of an Early Italian artist, and for the same reason, I surmised—the simplest, clearest and, in fact, probably the only way that either he or I could visualize them. I looked around for more paintings containing rocks and found two others, one of which had parts so identical with my latest pencil drawing of rocks, having even a certain new variation of indentation I had just worked out, that it was actually exciting. It is strange that this could excite me to the extent it did, but it was as if I had experienced an insight into the mind of an artist living over five hundred years ago. I knew why he had made these particular indentations to bring out his idea of a rocky surface, and knowing this, I felt a small bond with him—a bond that comes with having experienced in minute part similar artistic problems.

"By now this room, which only a few minutes before had held such little meaning, suddenly took on new light, and with eagerness I looked for more objects I could understand. There were no more paintings containing rocks, but it occurred to me that if the artists were on a level in which they painted rocks like mine, there must be other aspects in their works I could grasp. It took me some time, but gradually in this and subsequent visits to the museum I found more and more I could understand, not only in the room of the Early Italians, but in other rooms as well.

"To elaborate on some of my observations, I shall begin with a detailed description of one of the paintings called 'The Crucifixion,' according to the museum's information possibly done by Francesco Pesellino, 1422–1457, Italian School of Florence [picture 101], to which I returned over and over again with notebook and pencil. The Christ figure, raised high on a cross in the center of the painting, stands out clearly as the focal interest. Not only is this result further achieved by the contrast of His light upper body against the dark blue sky, but also in contrast to the three figures which are heavily and brightly robed. The grouping of the figures at the foot of the cross, whom I imagine to be the Virgin Mary on the left side, St. John on the right, and Mary Magdalene kneeling below and looking up, likewise directs the major interest to the Christ figure. Furthermore, while the landscape enriches the contents by giving the painting great depth, it does not detract from the central theme. In the first place, the horizon is low so that the mountains and trees do not interfere with the principal object—the Christ figure (probably for the same reason that I made the houses low so that they would not interfere with the head of the Negro boy). And secondly, the landscape further emphasizes the importance of the figures by the fact that the trees are small in comparison to the figures (again as I had made the trees small in comparison to my boy).

"Throughout the whole painting the artist had used the principle of bringing out objects against contrasting shades of light or dark (which I first consciously developed in my 'Cow Lost in the Woods' and have used as a fundamental principle in all my other paintings). He made the lower sky light so that the mountains, trees, and two standing figures could be brought out as

101. "The Crucifixion," by Francesco Pesellino, 1422–1457, Italian School of Florence.

clearly against it as the cross and the light upper body of the Christ figure were brought out against the dark blue upper sky. The same relationship is apparent across the whole painting. First, to the left the rocks are dark to set off the light blue robe of the Virgin Mary, which in turn is dark blue on the other side (to give the figure roundness) against light rocks. The light red robe of the Mary Magdalene figure is brought out clearly against the dark planes of the rocks, and again the dark rocks set off the light red robe of the St. John figure, which is also darkened on the other side against light rocks. Furthermore, the same principle is used in the formation of the rocks and robes to show clearly their characteristics: the alternating planes of light against dark are made to emphasize the stiffness of the rocks, while the dark (and therefore deep) folds are made to emphasize the quality and movement of the robes. Even in the faces I observed the same use of contrasting shades of light and dark to emphasize the features and expression. In the St. John figure, for example, the bowed head with the light chin against the dark side of the neck, the light nose and parted lips against the dark side of the face, the dark drawn eyebrows against the light forehead, combined to give the clear expression of anguish. In other words, the entire painting is based on this principle, in its details as well as in its whole construction. It is an artistic formation through which the artist expressed his religious feelings—and it is the same formation I am trying so hard to master. This fact in itself was of great interest to me, for I saw not only how the form gives clarity and strength to the contents, but I also saw how it makes the painting a work of art.

"This long and labored observation of Pesellino's painting has in itself been of help to me, both because it has furthered my ability to appreciate works of art and because it has stimulated me and given me new ideas for carrying out my knowledge of the artistic form to more advanced applications, particularly in relation to the painting of landscapes.

"However, with respect to the other Early Italian paintings I observed, I shall only briefly describe some additional aspects and principles I recognized. I noted in most of the Early Italian paintings—such as works of Daddi, De Freidi, Sassetta, to mention only a few—that in groups of objects which overlapped, as human figures standing side by side or horses lined up together, each figure was painted with a different-colored robe and each horse in a different color to distinguish clearly one from the other at the points of overlapping. I recognized in this the principle I had used (though I was by no means aware of its being a principle at the time) in making the sleeves of the farmer's wife light blue against her dark blue dress, as I then knew no other way to set them clearly off from each other.

102. "The Rustic Concert," Italian School of Florence, early fifteenth century.

"In a painting called 'The Rustic Concert', Italian School of Florence, early fifteenth century [picture 102], I observed another application of this same principle where outlined hills are distinguished from each other by different colors (as the outlined hills in my 'Bringing Home the Hay', in which I had given each hill a different shade of green, knowing no other way of distinguishing them). The trees in this painting are also outlined (as in several other Early Italian paintings) quite similarly to my outlined trees in 'Cow Lost in the Woods' and to the haystacks in my 'Farmer and Wife with Their Cow'. It seemed obvious to me why the artist had made that type of tree, namely, to avoid the confusion of overlapping leaves and branches. The grass and flowers are placed on lines, some of which appeared as mound tops, some as earth cracks, and others just lines—evidently for the same reason as I drew lines under the grass in 'Bringing Home the Hay'—to fasten the objects down and to keep them from floating. (I found this same type of base line, if one may call it that, in a number of the other paintings too. In 'The Nativity' by Fungai, Italian School of Sienna, 1460–1516, for example, all the people, horses, and even trees are placed on lines, such as darkened hilltops, as in my 'Cow Lost in the Woods', not only to fasten them down, but to make them stand out more clearly against the light of the next earth formation.) There is one aspect in 'Rustic Concert' which I did not see in the other paintings, and that is a certain unevenness in the formation of objects. Parts, such as the seated lady in the foreground and the rocklike hill to the left, seem more advanced than the rest of the objects, giving me the impression that the artist may have worked out new artistic forms in the process of painting, the principle of which he no doubt carried over into subsequent works.

"But merely mentioning these things that I noted does not bring out the personal identification I felt with the artists. By using the word identification, which may seem conceited and even absurd, I do not mean to imply that I feel I am nearing their heights or that my prosaic themes can be compared to their great religious paintings. I mean, rather, that I clearly understand them, for even though we speak of different things and my vocabulary is much inferior to theirs, we speak the same artistic language.

"In a room containing Flemish tapestries [picture 103] of the late fifteenth century, I was instantly at ease. The ground in these tapestries is represented throughout by overlapping mound formations in which the dark top of one stands out against the light base of another, and vice versa. Grass and flowers are consequently dark or light in accordance with the opposing light or dark of the earth formations, just as I had done in 'Cow Lost in the Woods'. The overlappings in the human figures and in the bodies of the animals are also carried out in the same way.

"Encouraged by my new abilities to appreciate works of art, I tried my knowledge on more modern artists. In a painting by Henri Rousseau called

103. Flemish tapestry of about 1500 A.D.

'Tropics' in which he had given light edges to his leaves to set them off from the adjoining leaves at the points of overlapping, I easily recognized the principle on which I had constructed the bushes and trees of my 'Negro Boy'. Despite the many overlappings in this painting, there is no confusion. I was also able to appreciate the striking clarity in Amedeo Modegliani's painting,

104. "La Colline des Pauvres," by Paul Cézanne.

'Red Head', which with its simple outlined face and neck against an almost even-colored background reminded me of my 'Negro Woman'. Previously I had passed it by as 'ugly': now I see it as a work of art—a strong, simplified impression of a woman.

"I stopped long before 'La Colline des Pauvres' by Paul Cézanne. [Picture 104.] Well acquainted with his great reputation, but not having appreciated him in the slightest, I could never understand why Cézanne was so highly esteemed. Once when I observed his paintings with a friend who was tremendously interested and enthusiastically appreciative, I felt (plus, of course, that usual backache) humiliated that I was so lacking in sensitivity or good taste, that I was completely blind to what those of 'culture' saw in Cezanne. Now I was determined to discover some spark of appreciation at least. I looked and waited long, but just as I was about to turn away still unhappily indifferent, a sudden recognition flashed through my mind. In the whole formation of his landscape—though his technique, colors, and representation of rocks and trees were beyond my ability to understand—I realized that he had used the same principle of dark and light to form his rocks and tree trunks. It was one of the fundamental artistic problems I actually understood, but hadn't recognized at first. This discovery of my own was as if I had received a present, for I felt in that joy of recognition that I was at last approaching an understanding of a work of art."

The uniqueness of this understanding of essential aspects of works of art lies in the fact that it is principally concerned with objective, artistic data. Miss E's critical observation is not characterized by explicative comments on line, color, composition, and so forth, based on ready-made "aesthetic hypotheses," which rarely touch the artistic problem that constitutes a work of art. The specific value of her approach is marked by precise visual judgment which arises from her own creative experience, that which in turn leads to the discovery of decisive pictorial functions, to principles of artistic configuration. This was best expressed when she became aware of the "light and dark" effect in "The Crucifixion" attributed to Pesellino: "the entire painting is based on this principle, in its details as well as in its whole construction." Miss E thus experienced, as she herself stated, "an insight into the mind of an artist living over five hundred years ago." And further, she has grasped the truth that this principle is an intrinsic factor of "an artistic formation through which the artist expressed his religious feelings." Therefore, she does not comprehend a work of art as mere "composition," meaning an arrangement of objects designed for "visual comfort," but as essential to the logic of a given content. This creative approach which reveals the connection between the artist's inner mental process and the realization of his ideas in his work has not only furthered the ability to appreciate works of art, but has become also an important incentive for the production of new, more advanced applications of the specific principle in relation to the painting of landscapes.

Miss E's report about her direct approach to an understanding of some essential aspects of old as well as modern works of art finds an extension in her evaluation of the social implications arising from the unfolding of her artistic energies.

"In concluding this report, which is to be my final one, I should like to say a word about the social implications of artistic activity—that aspect of the course which first drew me to it. Naturally, I see the implications in terms of my own experience and therefore I shall limit myself to a brief summary of what this course has meant to me. Primarily, I have found that life is richer since I began the work—richer in two respects. Not only have I a vital hobby that yields tremendous satisfactions in the process of work as well as in the feeling of accomplishment, but I see the world differently. I observe nature in a different and clearer light, with deeper appreciation for colors, movements, shapes, and the sweep of the whole. I observe our city streets and their jumbled buildings more clearly too, but with greater intolerance for their ugliness and the disorderly planning they point to. I observe—but perhaps it is enough to say I observe much, much more than I did before. In other words, as I developed a richer inner world I became more critically aware of the outer world. Difficult as it is to describe the effect of this double enrichment on my personality, I can definitely say I am more fully awake to my surroundings, more fully alive. Multiply this effect on one average individual by only a small fraction of the population, and the social implications of artistic activity seem clearly self-evident."

Pictures 105–109, on the following pages, show accomplishments of other members of the same group.

105. "Relief of a cat," chiseled in plaster of Paris and cast in artificial stone (15 by 20 inches), done by Mr. G. El, a broker twenty-nine years of age, after five months of participation in the course. Mr. El started with very simple drawings of horses which showed in their pictorial formation the greatest contrast of direction of lines. Gradually he developed them to more differentiated forms. After having been in the course two months, he was able to cut a relief of a structurally complicated "walking horse between two trees" in plaster of Paris, and achieved a complete unity of form. He cultivated his artistic ability by making a great number of drawings of his subjects until he could visualize his ideas. This work, which shows the visualization of the total figure of a cat, is nowhere distorted by incoherent, unessential details. It thus attains a monumental form that is the unadulterated result of his visual conception.

106. Portrait in relief, first modeled in clay and later cast in artificial stone (14 by 9 inches), also done by Mr. G. El after two years in the course. This portrait was not done from a model. In order to reach a convincing outline of this head Mr. El made many drawings. Finally he modeled his subject in clay on a plate of glass. The modeling of the differentiated outline of the face, as well as that of nose and mouth, is in contrast to the still flat, linear quality of the eye and hair. Thus the relief reveals a typical transition stage. However, the fact that this work could have been achieved without a model may indicate to what high artistic level a layman can cultivate his creative potentialities.

107. "My Garden in Kansas," a watercolor (14 by 22 inches) by Mrs. M. S., a nursery-school teacher fifty-four years of age.

Mrs. S's main interest revolved around rich recollections of her Kansas home, whence she had just come when she began the course. After she was able to draw and paint trees and flowers in a simple way, she displayed unusual energy and perseverance in the execution of details. However, through the development of her critical awareness she avoided pictorial disorder.

This watercolor shows in the formation of the hills spatial depth in accordance with an emphasized borderless transition from parts with figural meaning to parts with ground meaning. An application of this principle of form in the relationship of the manifold trees and flowers would have required a very high degree of visual conceiving. Consequently, they were formed according to an earlier stage, that of the variability of direction of lines. This stage also underlies the construction of the bench. (See the similar bench in picture 68.)

Despite the many details, a definite arrangement of trees and flowers and a clear organization of the figure-ground relationship of all parts, supported by different colors, has been achieved. The picture is thus far removed from naturalistic imitation. It is an orderly expression of a sensitive nature.

108. Painting of a woman (oil, 33 by 28 inches) done by Mrs. F. S., a former college instructor and at present a housewife, thirty-seven years of age. Mrs. S began her artistic activity by drawing trees and flowers in a simple way. She accomplished this imaginative painting after one year of participation in the course. The unified expression in all outlines of this figure, its total visualization based upon a distinct figure-ground relationship of head and body against the background, and of light lower arms against the dark body, and finally a harmonious color relationship of different color tones, make this work a pictorial whole.

109. "Woman with Scarf in Landscape" (oil, 32 by 28 inches) done by Mrs. F. S. after three years in the course. A close observation of the organization of form reveals a stage of development of artistic conceiving similar to that seen in Miss E's painting of a Negro boy. There is the same distinct figure-ground relationship of all the parts, a variability of direction of lines, and the same idea of spatial depth. However, in spite of these basic pictorial conformities, all contours of this picture show a more differentiated but harmonious application of the variability of direction of lines and a greater differentiation in the relationship of color tones. Thus a particular sensitivity of the creator is reflected, which leads to the realization of her personal style of expression.

Review and Summation

Chapter Seven

CONCLUSIONS FROM THE EXPERIMENT

I N THE LIGHT of the experience gained in the various projects, conclusions and their implications with reference to different social and educational activities seem warranted. Specific conclusions as they relate to the separate groups selected for the experiment, whose artistic productions we have reviewed, will be discussed first, before we proceed to the general conclusions.

MENTALLY DEFECTIVE PERSONS

The Southbury experiment seems to confirm the fact that creative activity in the visual arts can be unfolded and developed in mentally defective persons to a degree analogous to that of their mental potentialities.[1] Real difficulties appeared usually only with individuals with higher I.Q's who had previously received art instruction based on copying. With such a background, feeble-minded persons cling to a technique and slavish imitation which are in no way related to their stage of visual comprehension. Nevertheless, the imitative, memorized picture seems to give them a certain security. Any attempt to lead such persons back to their own stage of visual conceiving is usually resented vigorously because of their anxiety over losing that sterile mental possession and being thrown back into a state of uncertainty. The majority of children, however, were not influenced by any previous art teaching. For the awakening of their independent pictorial activity a knowledge of their mental peculiarities was indispensable.

Studies have shown that the mentally defective person operates most efficiently in a situation involving concrete, tangible things—that is, in direct sensuous experience. The pedagogical approach described in the Southbury experiment was in conformity with this particular mental attitude. Stimula-

---

[1] The neurological and psychological examinations of the children in the Southbury experiment did not reveal indications of brain pathology. The writer is therefore assuming that the conclusions to be presented have bearing only on the nonpathological type of defective individual.

tion for visually organized expression excluded, therefore, as much abstract conceptual activity as possible. To have asked such individuals to illustrate pictorially a given story or personal experience, even of the simplest kind, would have required a special mental reconstruction which might have been beyond their mental grasp. Furthermore, the fact of suddenly being faced with so abstract a task might have thrown them into a state of inner help- lessness. Difficulties were avoided by showing these feeble-minded persons color drawings which in their simple subject matter, as well as in their structural form, came very close to the stage of their own ability of visual comprehension. This directness of understanding gave satisfaction and joy, and prepared the awakening of their own pictorial activity. They accepted without hesitation the suggestion to make similar pictures. An immediate visual experience—a concrete experience—stimulated them to their first spon- taneous pictorial activity.

The restricted 'span of perseverance and lack of concentration of most feeble-minded persons were present in these children and proved great ob- stacles in the execution of their work. These characteristics were especially accentuated in the performance of an activity that was new to them. To reduce the difficulties, it was essential to limit the subject matter of representation and to employ very simple techniques and media. Plain forms of trees, flowers, animals, and other objects, clearly organized, gave great pleasure to these persons who had never before experienced the results of their own creative powers. To strengthen their belief in themselves, it was important to approve their achievements and to acknowledge their work. Convincing evidence of their progress was given them by showing them frequently the progressive sequence of their own accomplishments. With the growing satisfaction in their work, their faith in themselves increased, and consequently their per- severance and concentration. Finally, they were able to keep at their work with sustained interest for several hours.

The development of the artistic ability of these patients was primarily based on their own visual judgment of their finished works. After a short period of organized visual activity, a sensitivity for simple visual organization became evident. It was most apparent when a color drawing tended to result in a confusion, which always meant that their stage of visual conception was not realized. When that condition obtained, an uneasiness and inner discord gripped them, a mental state which usually resulted in great embarrassment:

faster breathing and nervous tension frequently appeared. By some of them this state was verbally expressed in simple terms, as, "I don't like it"; but by others, with a higher mentality, it was expressed in words indicating that they had reached a decision; they would say, "I can do it better." Stimulation to make their work "better" was always supported by their own desire to re-establish a visual order, either by correcting the color drawing or by starting a new work. Behavior of that kind had its origin in a need for regaining inner balance. Thus, visual judgment assisted the integration of personality.

The pedagogical procedure of the Southbury experiment took into full account the described mental characteristics of the feeble-minded persons. As a consequence, within their restricted mental capacities, they were able to develop an activity which created a well-organized pictorial production. The decisive significance of this process is that it involved in an integral way many different aspects of human functioning. By their own determining of their subject matter, manipulating their material, deciding to correct their dis-ordered works, and carrying out their task to the end, there emerged directed conceptual thinking, initiative, and perseverance. By their choosing their colors and enjoying them in a configurated structural whole their emotional experience became overtly expressed in a disciplined way. By establishing in all their works a logical construction of form—the artistic form, regardless of how simple it may have been—they performed a spontaneous mental act ade-quate to their potentialities. Furthermore, this act called forth a definite reor-ganization of their physical behavior: it affected their entire mental and physical nature. Finally, a development of their mental activity became mani-fest through the gradual accomplishment of more differentiated and more ex-tended tasks. Thus, a growth of personality had taken place which showed itself, in some patients, in a more mature, more disciplined behavior.

The Southbury experiment seems to substantiate the fact that artistic ac-tivity as the pictorial realization of inherent processes of visual conception, though functioning in a modest degree, may be of decisive significance in the education of mentally defective individuals. As we have noted earlier, its specific effect upon feeble-minded persons is based upon an intimate coördi-nation of functioning which operates predominantly in the realm of concrete experience. Such concrete experience leads toward creative formation of order and organization. "Order and organization is abstraction,"[2] irrespective of the

---

[2] Martin Schütze, *An Approach to the Understanding of Art* (Woodstock, New York, 1939).

field of experience in which it is performed. Creating order and organization in the realm of concrete, visual experience is a discipline thoroughly suited to the nature of mentally defective individuals which integrates their restricted capacities. Special education aiming at the unfolding of latent mental forces should make artistic activity an indispensable factor in daily instruction. As a fundamental pedagogical principle involving visual cognition it should attain even a primary place in everyday school work.

Besides being taught as an independent subject, "Art" should also be applied to other activities and subjects, such as reading, geography, or history, and in special projects. As a prerequisite for the fruitful success of this educational task it will also be necessary to limit a specific theme to such a degree that it can be easily grasped; that is, the subject matter should by no means require any complicated effort of thought for its understanding, but should be in the realm of immediate comprehension. Under such circumstances the mental capacities of the feeble-minded individual can operate uniformly.[3] Greater differentiation of visual conception makes possible more complicated abstract thinking about subject matter. To give an example: A child draws a tree showing only a vertical line for the trunk, and a few other lines connected with the trunk by either horizontal or slanting lines indicating the two different stages of the greatest contrast of direction or variability of direction. (See picture 3.) After his own spontaneous observation and judgment, or after being stimulated to "make it better," he may feel a need of repeating the rhythm of the vertical and horizontal or slanting branches and to apply the same relationship of form (the angle of connection) to smaller lines attached to the branches. Thus, the structural form is extended, with the effect that the shape of the tree becomes more differentiated (see picture 4). It must be emphasized, however, that the creation of this more complicated form of a tree does not result from the mere fact of knowing that a tree has many branches, because the possession of such abstract knowledge cannot explain the more extended unity of form in such a tree. It is the independent visual "feeling" for a greater extension in the integration of form that creates a greater visual comprehension of the tree. Out of this a more complicated abstract understanding of that tree enters the consciousness of the child. Thus, visual conception precedes and determines the formation of abstract concepts. In this way, a natural transition from concrete behavior to abstract thought

---

[3] It is obvious that these pedagogical suggestions are also basic in the education of normal children.

takes place. The process of such growth may be very slow—as is the mental growth of feeble-minded individuals in general,—but since it is thoroughly sound it is not only pedagogically justified but also pedagogically obligatory.

The experiment involving several mentally deficient children in coöperative work is of particular importance. It has to be noted that coöperative effort is only possible if the persons selected for the experiment are at the same stage of development of visual conception, for only this condition guarantees a shared understanding of their work. The restricted mentality of feeble-minded individuals prevents them from being fluently communicative; some even tend toward shyness which easily leads them into a state of isolation. In coöperative work, as described earlier, all members are bound to the success of the entire task, because only within the total design does the drawing of each member receive its value. The awareness of this fact compels them to participation in the procedure of the whole work and in this way they necessarily become involved in an exchange of opinion. The essence of such coöperative endeavor forces the participants to give up their attitudes of withdrawal because only in the successfully organized total work can their contributions exist. This condition calls forth a group responsibility, a community spirit, which in turn gives to the participating individual the feeling of human worth, the consciousness of being recognized as a decisive factor in the group and community.

The unfolding of inherent artistic abilities, as has been shown in Selma's case, may also be of value in its application to the schooling of those feeble-minded children whose instruction takes place primarily in so-called "Industrial Training Units." These patients, who are taught embroidery, weaving, rugmaking, and the like, often surprise one with the accurateness of their work, in spite of the fact that the pictorial designs given to them for execution are often far above their own abilities of visual comprehension and alien to them. If one takes into consideration how easily persons who are mentally defective fall into mechanical manual operation, any prescribed manipulation—performed under strict supervision—can reach remarkable results in skill. From a pedagogical viewpoint, however, which aims at a harmonious unfolding of general human functions, in which the nature of the individual determines the educational course, the most skillful accomplishments lose their apparent significance if they are not inwardly related to the producer himself. The Southbury experiment seems to have demonstrated that an intimate connection between work and producer can be established. Children working in Industrial Training Units have enough perceptual abilities to create their own simple but genuine designs. Always, when the applied designs were self-developed products, the patients manifested a definite eagerness linked with a constant interest in their task. Working on this basis, they displayed unusual perseverance and steadiness, sometimes over a period of weeks, which indicated a definite tendency toward self-directed activity.

Most of the mentally defective spent many years in institutions, and some even their whole lives. For the establishment of normal and healthy conditions through which these patients may receive their inner security, their surroundings should be shaped as much as possible to accord with their specific nature. "Only when the world is adequate to man's nature do we find what we call security." If this is true of the person who has normal powers of adjustment, how much more necessary is a suitable environment for the mental defective, who surrenders easily to inadequate situations. Since it seems possible that most feeble-minded children are able to give forms of their own devising to embroideries, rugs, weavings, and the like, a varied opportunity exists of permitting them to determine the character of their environment. For the sake of their inner stability and satisfaction, for the sake of their own enjoyment in the realization of their own world, they should be led to create their own cultural pattern. The formation of such a "culture" would not force them into isolation from the world of normal man. There are vast regions of folk art as well as of primitive art which speak a language of form similar to that of genuine works of the feeble-minded. There are ample possibilities of fostering a mental enrichment of such institutionalized persons by acquainting them with works of handicraft and arts which express a related stage of visual conception.

Administrators of such institutions often have to consider selling the products of Industrial Training Units to the public in order to obtain some self-support. The executives may be reminded that they face a responsible cultural task. On the one hand, they can call forth an increase in the amount of trash if they let the instructors of the Industrial Training Units orient their taste to suit the demands of the general public, while at the same time the "producing" inmates are driven deeper into mental confusion and rigidity because the work they have to do goes against their entire nature. The financial sup-

---

[4] Kurt Goldstein, *Human Nature* (Harvard University Press, 1940), p. 112.

port may be successful, business may flourish, but the invisible result is destruction of irreparable human values. On the other hand, the understanding of simple, good handicrafts is growing rapidly. The unadulterated plainness of the works of mentally deficient persons may well find their place and usefulness in homes of cultivated taste. Thus, the modest artistic work of feeble-minded individuals can contribute its share to the rebuilding of a general artistic culture, simpler but nearer to human nature though it may be. Under such circumstances, business for self-support becomes morally fully justified.

The demonstrated artistic development of Selma reveals, besides its educational success, definite therapeutic implications. In effect, a retarded and insecure individual of thirty, with a high degree of anxiety and inability to find her place, established an adequate attitude to life. This therapeutic result could not have been reached by a mere release of pent-up energies, as is usually attempted by expressive methods such as finger painting. Approaches of this type may throw light upon the psychological and psychiatric peculiarities of the patient under observation. They may help free him from emotional inhibitions. But such methods of mere expression are hardly beneficial when primary concern is for the fundamental rebuilding of a personality. For this purpose, constructive results can only be achieved by the awakening of a formative activity which affects the individual dynamically as a psychophysical whole. Artistic activity—as the pictorial realization of inherent evolutionary processes of visual conceiving—acts in such a way. Irrespective of the modest accomplishments it may produce when applied in special education, it not only releases repressed inner forces, but brings into intimate coördination all essential aspects of human functioning. It organizes and forms in an all-embracing normal operation the total entity of the patient. He witnesses his own spontaneous development. Step by step he "masters" more extended tasks. His belief in himself and his self-respect increase gradually. In this way artistic activity attains the meaning of a psychotherapy.

The application of artistic activity—as understood in this approach—may also result in a special contribution to occupational therapy, especially if it is concerned with restoration of disabled organs or remobilizing of diseased parts. Such organs, for instance, as hands, arms, and fingers are often treated separately, isolated from their natural adjustment with the individual as a whole. Under such conditions the patient is compelled to focus his interest mainly on his disability. The detached parts may gain an abnormal prominence. Through constant attention to a single stimulus the person under treatment can develop an unnatural rigidity. This attitude may even find its expression in nervous and mental tensions that might sometimes explode and cause violent acts. Restoration and healing are thus frequently disturbed.[5] The disturbance can be neutralized if the divorced function of an organ becomes part of a process that involves the patient as a unified organism. It is in this particular relation to occupational therapy that artistic activity can be of decisive importance. To give an example: where the functions of arms, hands, or fingers have to be remobilized, and weaving, carving, drawing, and the like, have been considered as applicable for this purpose, the pictorial idea to be realized should be primarily the patient's own. Once the idea is his, a persistent interest in the execution of the artistic task is usually guaranteed. It has previously been indicated that within the course of such artistic activity each decisive stroke, bit of modeling, use of color the functional meaning of which within the structural order of form is thoroughly determined by the stage of visual conceiving requires a high degree of motor control. It has also been noted that "the average state of tension of the single muscle is not determined by the muscle alone, but by the situation of the whole of the organism."[6] This means that the act of remobilizing an arm or parts of it is no longer divorced from feeling, visual conception, and the physical behavior of the rest of the body. The interest of the patient is concentrated on the procedure and development of his work. The organ to be rehabilitated does not gain predominance. Instead of rigidity, a flexible attitude and constant equalization in all actions are attained. The therapeutic process becomes an intrinsic part of an activity embracing many essential aspects of human nature. Artistic activity obtains the function of a creative therapy.

The application of artistic activity in its therapeutic sense goes far beyond the sphere of special education. In a world in which millions of persons, civilians as well as soldiers, are shocked by the various effects of war, in which thousands are ill from having been worn out by too severe compulsory work, the restoration and equalization of minds and bodies have become fundamental tasks. In such undertakings artistic activity can only be of constructive value when it stems from human experience and when it operates as an in-

---

[5] Kurt Goldstein explains this as "the consequence of a disturbance of the normal figure-ground process" within the functioning of the human organism, considering the isolated organ as figure and the rest of the body as ground. See more about this problem in his book, *Human Nature*, pp. 12–19.

[6] *Ibid.*, p. 124.

herent process of man's being. It should, therefore, be clear that any imposed method of art teaching, or leaving the individual alone so that he is forced to utilize only his reproductive memory, does not activate his spontaneous creativity. Through such approaches mind, body, and its parts are split into isolated potencies. As a consequence, harmonious functions of energies cannot take place. Thus, genuine artistic results are not achieved and therapeutic value can hardly exist. The reaction of the convalescent is usually an abnormal strain which may end in aversion to work. This is particularly evident when patients are aware that what they are doing is mainly "to be kept busy and active in something that somebody thinks is good for them." Few self-respecting persons like to be industrious in what they feel is "made work." Artistic activity, in order to lead to a successful therapeutic outcome, requires, in addition to the adequate application of the right tools and techniques, the focusing of attention on the unadulterated creative process. The individual has to be led to his particular stage of visual conceiving. Progress is based upon his own visual judgment and comprehension of his work as a pictorially formed whole. Stimulation can be given by showing the patient works of art and handicraft which in their construction of form are related to his own stage of visual comprehension. Being active in this way means that all manipulations of the organ under treatment are regulated from within. The patient's total organism participates. It seems obvious that through a process so versatile the therapeutic effect and the artistic quality of the attained work—simple though it may be—are inseparably bound together.

DELINQUENTS

The experiment with delinquents leads, in general, to similar conclusions. Most of the boys assigned to the project at New Hampton were considered by psychological and educational tests to be below normal. The majority displayed mental attitudes similar to those of feeble-minded persons. It is therefore obvious that in the educational treatment of delinquent individuals who are below normal an approach may be undertaken similar to that taken with the feeble-minded. The delinquent boys with more highly developed mental potentialities proceeded in their work almost in the same way as the two we have discussed from the group of refugees and business and professional people. Consequently their achievements were higher with respect to more differentiated stages of visual conceiving.

Most of the participants in the New Hampton experiment were very undeveloped individuals. Poverty and unemployment were their background, and their hardships had apparently driven them into a state of mind which sought satisfaction of their crudest needs and left them indifferent to cultivated interests. In some, this condition was further intensified by their realization that after their release from the penalty imposed on them a basic change would be improbable. These circumstances may explain why most of the boys displayed an estranged attitude or even an unwillingness to do anything, at the beginning of the course. They were not able to understand how they could be active in art. The idea that they could do creative work was therefore jokingly dismissed, rather than accepted with interest or pleasure. A few of the boys, in their efforts to maintain their complete lack of interest and inability, even refused to be stimulated at all.

After some of the boys had started and had displayed progress in their work, the others evidently felt a little embarrassed. As they did not want to be idle, they soon voluntarily made first attempts at scribbling. When it was suggested to them that they should judge their finished drawings or modelings from a distance, and in accordance with their own feeling, and that they should then decide about how to proceed with a new work, the entire group gradually became busy. It was revealing to observe how these boys, because of their very lack of interest in nature, reached simple, though clear, structural formations in their pictorial results. Yet these results were so closely related to their visual comprehension that they received from them a definite satisfaction. For instance, a boy of eighteen, with the lowest intelligence quotient in the group, who drew a cow exactly horizontal and vertical became so excited about his picture that he repeatedly said, "That looks like a real cow."

To be active in this way soon removed their doubts of their creative abilities. And when, after a week, their primitive results could be compared with similar stages of artistic production from early epochs, in works of primitive or folk art, remarks like "I never thought that I could do that" were often heard. Step by step these boys became aware of the importance of their work for their own enjoyment. They showed one another their achievements, received praise from one another, accepted and gave advice. Discussions opened concerning problems which none of them had ever before thought about. They wanted to know more about art, about the origin of the works with which their own had been compared. Not one boy failed to develop his innate artistic activity in keeping with his natural potentialities. This success in turn stimulated them to interest their friends outside the group, and in time many other boys inquired if they could be assigned to the project.

The experience gained in the two days weekly which were given to the work made itself felt throughout the rest of the week. The productive effort, modest as it may seem to other people, forced these boys to further endeavors. After six o'clock in the evening, when they entered their cells, some of them frequently continued their work by making sketches for new paintings or sculptures. Others cut from old magazines photographs of works of art which they either wanted to have explained or which had some relation to their own achievements. The newly gained consciousness of doing something creatively, something they never had expected to be able to do, made them proud of themselves. Feelings of inferiority slowly retreated from their minds; faith and self-respect became more dominant. This change found its best expression in their letters to relatives and friends.

The New Hampton experiment, in which the majority of participants were below the average in mentality, throws light on the fundamental relationship of artistic activity to the nature of man. The fact that all the boys could be led to develop their creative existence may open new ways for the education, adjustment, and rehabilitation of institutionalized delinquents.

Since most inmates of reformatories cannot—according to their minor offenses—be considered as dangerous criminals, such institutions should appear less as places of punishment and more as places of opportunity to awaken the "better nature" in the consciousness of their inmates. This "better nature" emerges clearly during the process of the creative act. In the realization of his own visual conception the individual has to surrender himself to the unadulterated artistic process. No other idea, except that of giving full attention to perfecting the work under execution, dominates his mind. As this kind of production demands a highly disciplined function of thought and feeling as well as physical control, it brings the whole personality into a state in which he who creates becomes aware that the integration of his work requires the sacrifice of all other ideas which do not pertain to the creative process. It is this principal aspect of the artistic activity which contains the high ethical values of the devotion of self to the realization of the artistic form.

It belongs to the essence of many types of antisocial behavior that offenses are either committed without taking into consideration the welfare of others or are willfully directed to hurt others. The enjoyment of his own creative work produced by each member of a community leads spontaneously to an interest in the work of co-workers, especially when the results show a close relationship in their structural organization of form. Thus, the neighbor appears in the light of a productive being. In coöperative work, as has been demonstrated, all participants have to adjust themselves to one another for the sake of attaining the unified order of form in the whole design. In the flux of discussions about the progress of the common endeavor each individual learns to evaluate and appreciate the thoughts of others. Under such conditions, tolerance and respect for each one's opinion become indispensable. Experiences of this type within a productive community may become a necessary prerequisite for the rebuilding of the delinquent's future life.

Through the creation of his artistic production that carries the stamp of his personality the delinquent inevitably arouses the interest of others from whom he may receive appreciative acknowledgment of his work. In this way an awareness of his human worth may dawn in him. Furthermore, as he can witness the gradual progress in his performances, he may gain self-respect and faith in himself.

After the delinquent has been released from the reformatory, he takes something home with him that is really his own. One of the boys who participated in the New Hampton project wrote in a letter: "The work I do here gives me an idea for a hobby to pass the time away instead of hanging around the streets." Another boy, with a higher intelligence quotient, wrote: "I am happy to have learned as much as I did. Words cannot express my gratitude. I shall not forget it. If I am ever free again I shall continue my art work with much zeal." Statements such as these indicate that the unfolding of creative energies in visual art can have its effect beyond the doors of penal institutions. It may help the former delinquent to find his "better self" and prevent him from repeating his previous errors.

REFUGEES, AND BUSINESS AND PROFESSIONAL PEOPLE

From the four projects that have been demonstrated, the highest mental potentialities were found among the participants of the groups of refugees and of business and professional people. Here, the study may reveal to what unexpected artistic heights the layman can ascend when the art-educational method applied is based on the natural unfolding and growth of his artistic abilities. These results attain even greater significance if one realizes that they were performed in leisure hours and often after a long day of hard work. However, the fact that most of the students were still able to devote themselves to this new activity may indicate how much this work meant to them.

Some participants found the first steps into the field of creative activity in visual art difficult, but were able to proceed more easily by following the suggestion that they use only one medium and scribble or draw whatever came to mind. It was hard for them to reconcile their primitive beginnings with their knowledge of their subject matter. They were even embarrassed because they did so "poorly." But this discomfort was eased when it was explained to them that their results were as expected. Discussions threw light upon the fact that what they had just produced looked childish because their creative ability had never been developed beyond the stages of childhood. But so far as the first results truly reflected their genuine stage of artistic conceiving— primitive though it appeared,—a natural foundation was laid from which development could take place. Repeated advice to judge their finished work from a distance so that they could see their "ideas" more clearly, made them eager to make corrections and changes until they should reach a comprehensive picture of their subject. In effect, those first pictures became structurally organized in accordance with early stages of visual conceiving. Progress in this direction gave them the necessary impetus to continue without self-depreciation and reservations. Once accustomed to this procedure, most of the students showed a surprising ability to reach out for a definite visual order that was a result of their innate compulsion toward clear visual comprehension.

With their increasing power of visual discrimination the students revealed a growing ability to produce creative configuration. A few weeks after the beginning of these two projects with refugees and business and professional people, some of the students already felt encouraged to continue their work at home. Others did sketches for new ideas which they wanted to have discussed in the meetings.

Not all participants in these groups demonstrated, in their first pictorial attempts, unadulterated early stages of visual conceiving. Although a few of them began with undeveloped and even clumsy drawings, the confused shapes indicated that they intended to imitate complicated poses of objects. In other words, they tried to render their reproductive memory. They wanted to draw what they knew conceptually about their subject matter. Their efforts resulted in a patching together of incoherent details and produced a disorganized, confused representation. Advised to practice critical observation of their work, often supported by the introduction of different media, these students were led to early stages of visual conceiving pictorially realized in simple but genuine artistic formations. Once the natural basis or starting point had been reached, an organic unfolding and development to higher artistic stages began to take place.

There were, of course, ups and downs in all proceedings. Sometimes students achieved quick results, but often they struggled long before reaching a clear visual comprehension. There were pauses and interruptions, some caused by pressures of employment, some by the participants' need to adjust themselves to particularly difficult tasks. However, such suspension of activity sometimes seemed to be of value. The saying, "All things take time," applies to artistic activity also, and may even be of decisive importance. Since the pictorial result is the outcome of a creative process based upon mental growth, such pauses may be organic necessities. Inner preparation for attainment of a visual conception is obviously too much neglected in the practice of art education in special as well as in general schools.[7] Nevertheless, in the practice of the different experiments demonstrated in this book, such mental preparation favored by pauses and temporary suspensions of work seemed an important factor in a number of the achievements, and therefore were productive.

With growing maturity in their pictorial results—that is, with the attainment of a more complex visual order—greater concentration of all forces was required and the working processes inevitably slackened. It soon became obvious how creative work adequately suited to the mental stage of its producer can call forth unexpected powers. To these "laymen," life seemed to be vitally enriched. They experienced the rare pleasure of creation. They manifested a devotion to the completion of their task to the best of their abilities and consequently a work was not finished until it entirely satisfied them. The intelligent organization of the pictorial whole—this artistic perfection—became more and more their objective. The temporary "final" results ("final" until new artistic stages emerged) were the utmost realizations of their visual conception. The students were thus fully conscious that their achievements were wholly their own, and it was no accident, therefore, that none of them ever thought of signing his finished work.

---

[7] A case of such mental preparation is clearly demonstrated in Bruno Adriani's book, *Pegot Waring Stone Sculptures* (Nierendorf Editions, New York, 1945), pp. 15–17.

The devotion with which these persons participated in the experiments may throw some light upon the deep satisfaction that they received from their activity. Then satisfaction came from their awareness of the unfolding of their creative potentialities, of which they knew nothing before. It was further increased by the fact that they gradually became conscious—as frequently stated by themselves—of a unique cultivation of disciplined feeling and thinking, of an intimate coördination of mind, eye, and hand, as well as manual skill. They felt the formative effect which genuine artistic activity had upon them as assisting toward a more harmonized, more balanced personality.

The spontaneous critical judgment which mainly caused the organic development of these students' artistic abilities was gradually applied, also, to observation of their environment. They became seriously aware of the fact that the greater part of their surrounding world did not possess that basic visual order which was the decisive quality of their own achievements. The deformed shapes of buildings, the utterly incoherent architectural planning of streets and squares, previously ignored by most of them attracted their attention more and more. Simultaneously, they also became sensitive to the formless objects, the cheap as well as the expensive, displayed in shop windows. Instead of giving them visual satisfaction, such as they derived from the outcome of their own well-organized artistic works, the misshapen objects aroused in them feelings of irritation. Such annoyance, induced by the awakening of critical visual judgment, appeared to be a less desirable result of the unfolding of artistic potentialities. However, the experience had definite positive aspects. The idea dawned in most of these "laymen" that the present shape of their surrounding world must inevitably cause similar reactions upon every sensitive person and therefore should not be tolerated. Out of this experience serious efforts may develop to help toward changing and improving these conditions. When critical visual judgment, as the result of genuine artistic activity, leads to the knowledge of needed change and improvement of living conditions, it attains the utmost social importance.

GENERAL CONCLUSIONS

The entire experiment, in which persons of widely varied abilities, ages, and educational backgrounds were engaged, may throw light upon autonomous mental processes which until now have been too little recognized. It is through these processes that man is able to comprehend sensuously the appearances of the world and to express his comprehension symbolically by means of the artistic form. The demonstration, in which all participants developed their various degrees of artistic potentiality, may justify the assumption that the ability to create the artistic form by means of visual conceiving is a natural attribute of the mental existence of man. The origin of artistic production can therefore only be found in the spiritual being of man himself, specifically in a *definite* sensation and a *precise* feeling for form that is constantly governed by visual conceiving, which in turn is spontaneously realized by a self-sustained visual organization of form. Consequently, it seems impossible to attain the artistic form by advising students to compose a pictorial work according to special rules of outwardly predetermined pictorial effects. From the beginning on, such efforts exclude the individual's own spontaneous visual comprehension from the creative process and try to combine separated sensations and isolated experiences and thus conceptualize the sensuous creative processes. In effect, natural unfolding and development of artistic powers cannot take place. The entire experience reveals that, from the beginning, artistic activity is an autonomous operation, independent of conceptual calculation and abstract thinking, but based upon sensuous creation and "visual thinking" of relationships of form. Further, as a natural attribute of man's spiritual being, artistic activity should also be considered as a part of nature. Its growth can only take place in accordance with natural laws of unfolding and development; that is, as in the growth of all things in nature, simple structures precede more complicated ones. With respect to artistic activity, such growth functions naturally according to the evolutionary laws of visual conceiving. The incentive for such growth lies in the creator's innermost compulsion to proceed to a clearer and richer visual cognition by independent visual judgment of his work. Through this process each successive stage of artistic configuration prepares thoroughly the condition for the formation of the next stage. Art education which stands on such natural foundations becomes able to achieve results hitherto unexpected of the layman. Thus, it may become a decisive factor in the groundwork of a culture that rests on the creative nature of man.

The experiment reveals further that the natural unfolding of inherent artistic activity can take place only if its execution is suited to the individual's specific mental capacities and interests; that is to say, if it starts at the student's unadulterated stage of his visual conceiving.

In this way, the student's spiritual autonomy is recognized from the beginning on. The need for the pictorial realization of his own visual conception compels the individual to find and establish his own artistic standpoint. It inevitably requires an upright creative attitude, and in accomplishing an integrated organization of form it leads to artistic truth.

The independent process of striving for a definite order of form in the field of visual experience affects the individual as a psychophysical whole. Such striving helps to shape a more balanced personality by decisively furthering the organization or reorganization, the construction or reconstruction, of essential aspects of one's total functioning. These two ends point to basic educational values and far-reaching therapeutic implications. The results of such formative processes are of vital social importance in the present highly industrialized and mechanized civilization, in which, more than ever, man needs an equalizing force for the development of his whole being.

In the organic development and realization of visual conception, definite corresponding stages of artistic configuration in works of art of various epochs and races are reëxperienced. Consequently, a creative approach is made possible for a genuine understanding of related artistic productions. This approach neither underestimates the importance of a scientific explanation of historical, cultural, religious, or other aspects of works of art, nor minimizes an intelligent analysis of their composition for the purpose of gaining insight into their structural meaning. However, it emphasizes the fact that configurated visual experience through which a work of art has been conceived and brought forth cannot be replaced by conceptual comprehension. There is a great distinction between information about a thing and cognition of a thing: the one can be learned, the other can only be self-experienced. Through self-experienced understanding this creative approach establishes a mental tradition in works of art often far removed in time and space; it revitalizes them and may even give back to them an artistic mission in the fructification of new ideas.

In conclusion, the broadest implications of the unfolding of inherent artistic abilities can ultimately be attained only if one of the main obstacles for the development of a genuine artistic culture is removed. This obstacle consists in the common attitude that gives credit and acclaim predominantly to the artistic performance of talented persons. Fixed yardsticks of artistic judgment based upon various old and modern standards of criticism and used only for evaluating the works of "artists" have been unable to establish basic foundations for general objective artistic values. Thus the creativity of the great majority of people has been decisively obstructed. A just artistic evaluation of a work of art can only be concerned with artistic quality—the intelligent organization of form,—no matter how simple its structure may appear. In view of the findings of the entire experiment, in which all participants with their wide range of abilities could achieve genuine artistic results, it seems evident that the overstressed distinction between the artistic works of gifted and ungifted people is not of fundamental importance for the development of an artistic culture; whereas the application of an art-pedagogical principle which is able to unfold and to cultivate unadulterated artistic activity as an inherent attribute of human nature becomes of primary significance.

The necessity for reëvaluating the yardsticks used for discriminating the artistic works of gifted and ungifted people also finds support in the growth and decline of great artistic epochs, as, for instance, in the history of Europe. There it can clearly be observed how the creative energies of the people, manifested in a diversity of artistic expressions from modest pictorial formations to remarkable architectural structures, were the fundamental backbone of the artistic culture. It was also the same creative spirit which gave nourishing soil to the growth of the leading artist and which sustained him throughout his life. Unfortunately, with the beginning of the mechanized industrialization in the last century, in Europe as well as in America, quantity gradually displaced quality. The formative hands of the people became more and more superfluous. In turn, the general public lost its intimate relation to the artist. Thrown back on himself, isolated and misunderstood, he had to fight his lonely way. As he was unable alone to carry the artistic culture of his time, a decline of general standards of quality was inevitable. All efforts of the rising art-educational movements which followed either the trends of academic rules, or, later, the continually changing art vogues, fixed their main attention on the mass production of so-called "artists" and ignored a revitalization and dynamic participation of the creative powers of the people. Thus, the foundation for a unified artistic culture became impossible. Nevertheless, many efforts have been successfully undertaken to give a quality of form to many objects of practical use. But in view of the fact that the "unbearable visual squalor of Main Street" and the chaotic designs and shapes in most of our commodities still exist, individual and isolated efforts to raise the standards do not suffice. Further, if it is true that man by nature adjusts himself in time to most situations, it is alarming to think how such adjustments to deformed environments may so far lower the level of our present civilization that it may compare unfavorably with that of primitive people. To the American Indians, for example, the production of things for daily use had always been an artistic activity. In sum, neither the furtherance of only a minority of isolated and gifted artists nor the individual efforts of a few schools and private agencies can stem the tide of cultural decline. To call forth a basic change it will be necessary to awaken and activate the inherent creative potentialities of the mass of the people and to incorporate them in all constructive educational and social programs. This does not mean an artificial revitalization of folk art for which the spiritual foundations are no longer given. It means, rather, that even the modest, unadulterated creative processes of ordinary laymen become of ultimate importance, because they contain basic formative values which further critical visual discrimination and thus inevitably become incentives for altering a deformed environment into a visual coherent whole. Consequently, the overemphasized distinction between the works of gifted and of ungifted individuals has to be corrected, for it impedes the rise and the function of a general artistic culture.

There is no way of turning back the onward surge of mechanized industrialization. However, in its further development more and more free hours will gradually be gained. Inevitably, greater leisure will increase the need for a wisely directed outlet of energies. If most people continue to use free time predominantly for passive recreation there will be no essential benefit for either individual or society. It will be wise, therefore, to anticipate this problem by turning serious attention to the great opportunities for freeing active constructive forces pertaining to the very nature of artistic activity. For the sake of a profound universal effect such constructive forces should, of course, already be activated in early childhood. They should be developed organically through adolescence up to mature stages of adulthood. In this way the creative energies of the people will ultimately become a decisive factor in counteracting the dangers of modern mechanized life. Art education that recognizes artistic activity as a general attribute of human nature and that aims at the unfolding and developing of man's latent creative abilities will then contribute its share to the great task which faces all of us, the resurrection of a humanized world.

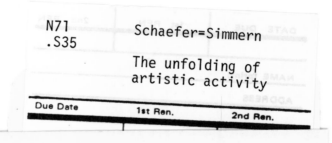